CHINESE CHESS

卒 卒 卒 炮 車 馬 象 士 将 士 象 馬 車 炮 卒 卒

CHINESE CHESS

兵 兵 兵 炮 車 馬 相 士 帥 士 相 馬 車 炮 兵 兵

by H. T. LAU

CHARLES E. TUTTLE COMPANY
Rutland · Vermont : Tokyo · Japan

REPRESENTATIVES

Continental Europe: BOXERBOOKS, INC., *Zurich*
British Isles: PRENTICE-HALL INTERNATIONAL, INC., *London*
Australasia: BOOK WISE (AUSTRALIA) PTY. LTD., *Sydney*
104–108 Sussex Street, Sydney 2000

Published by the Charles E. Tuttle Company, Inc.
of Rutland, Vermont and Tokyo, Japan
with editorial offices at
Suido 1-chome, 2–6, Bunkyo-ku, Tokyo

Library of Congress Catalog Card No. 84–052394
International Standard Book No. 0–8048 1495–3

First printing, 1985

Printed in Japan

· TABLE OF CONTENTS ·

· INTRODUCTION ·

The game of Chinese chess, known as "elephant chess" in Chinese, is played by Chinese the world over. Despite its wide popularity, however, it is very difficult to review the history and development of the game because of the lack of systematic literature. There is some evidence that it was imported from India in the second half of the first century A.D. At that time the board, pieces, and movement of the pieces were different from those of today. It was reported that in A.D. 839 the prime minister of the Tang dynasty (618–907) added two extra pieces called "cannon" to the game. By the end of the eleventh century, the game had evolved into the form which exists today.

Most of the writings on Chinese chess from early times have not been well preserved. Often for a book of, say, twelve volumes, only three of them are found, and many pages in those three volumes might be missing. Furthermore, the dates of the works and names of authors are often not known. Apparently, the earliest publication that still exists in its complete form today is one that dates from the Ming dynasty (1368–1644). It is a book with a collection of seventy short end-games and solutions published in 1522. A ten-volume book that is said to be the second oldest in the literature appeared in 1570.

The first eight volumes record 550 different end-games with solutions; the last two list some complete games.

A milestone was laid in 1632 when a book by Jin-zhen Zhu called *The Secret Inside the Orange,* the last book on Chinese chess to come out during the Ming dynasty, was published. It is said that the title of the book was derived from a legend:

> There was once an orange field in which an enormous orange was grown. When the orange was peeled, it was found that inside two old men were sitting facing each other, playing chess.

The book represents a summary of the remarkable accomplishments in the game before and throughout the Ming dynasty. The first two parts of the book record complete games, while the last two are a collection of 133 end-games. The examples of the complete games are a most valuable reference for beginners. Remarkable offensive strategies are demonstrated, each one using the most clear-cut possible steps to realize the defeat of the opponent. The moves are extremely elegant and easy to understand. The complete games are presented in Appendix 1 of the present work.

About sixty years after the appearance of *The Secret Inside the Orange,* at the end of the seventeenth century, a book of complete games called *The Plum-Blossom Meter* was written by Zai-yue Wang. The exact date of the work is not known. The original copy was hand-written and not printed, probably due to the financial condition of the author; the first printed edition appeared in 1917. The book presents a wide variety of systematically classified and carefully elaborated strategies, which should be studied by anyone who is serious about learning the game. The entire sets of moves from *The Plum-Blossom Meter* are listed in Appendix 2.

Although very few books on the subject of Chinese chess have appeared since the publication of the two books mentioned above, the game itself still retains a widespread popularity in Chinese communities around the world. Since most of what has been written on the subject has been in the Chinese language, however, the author hopes that the publication of this book will encourage an interest in Chinese chess among Western readers as well.

As a final note, the author would like to express his gratitude to Vaclav Chvátal, who has given continuous encouragement during the preparation of the book.

PART · 1 · THE BASICS

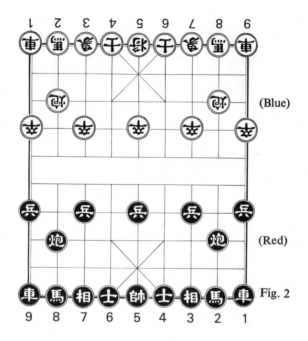

(Blue)

(Red)

Fig. 2

below. In the heading for the description of each piece, the following information is given: the piece and its corresponding Chinese character, with alternate forms in parentheses; the words "blue" or "red" in parentheses if the two sides have different characters for a piece of the same value; the English term for the piece; the abbreviation for the piece; the pronunciation of the Chinese character in the *pinyin* system of romanization; and the literal meaning of the character.

将 (將) (blue) **King (K)** *jiang,* general
帥 (red) **King (K)** *shuai,* general

The king is the most important piece. If the king is lost,

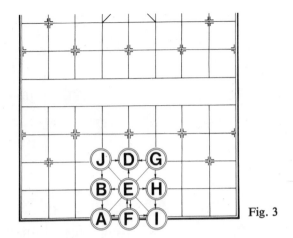

Fig. 3

so is the game. When the king comes under direct attack, it must be moved out of the line of attack in the next move, or the attacking piece must be blocked by one of the pieces on the king's side.

The king is allowed to move back and forth between positions A, B, J, D, E, F, G, H, and I—the "palace"—as shown in Figure 3. The king may move horizontally or vertically, but not diagonally, and only one space at a time. (Note that the two diagonal lines in the palace, found on all standard boards, are merely there to show where the palace is. They have nothing to do with the king's mode of movement.) The king may never move outside of his palace. For example, if the king is in position F, it can move to positions A, E, or I; if it is in position E, it can move to positions B, D, H, or F; if it is in position G, it can move to positions D or H. If one of the opponent's pieces is situated in a position where the king can move, the king can capture it.

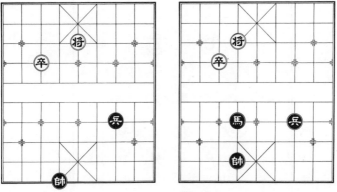

Fig. 4   Fig. 5

There is an exceptional rule regarding the king in Chinese chess: the two kings cannot be positioned on the same vertical line without any other piece between them. (In a sense, the king would be able to make a long jump and capture the other king if the two of them were so aligned.) Thus, in Figure 4, assuming that it is red's move, red's king may not move one space to the right. In Figure 5 (red's move), red cannot move its knight 馬, since doing so would bring the two opposing kings onto the same line without any other piece intervening.

車 Rook (R) *ju,* chariot

The rook's manner of movement is exactly the same as that of the rook in the Western chess game. It can travel horizontally or vertically, but not diagonally, to any position on the board (it can cross the river) as long as there is no obstruction in its path. It is able to capture any piece of the opponent's in its path.

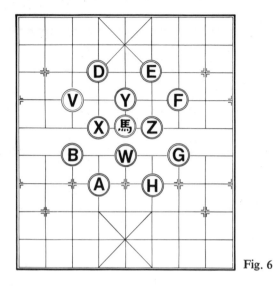

Fig. 6

⦿ 炮 **Cannon** (C) *pao,* cannon

There is no piece in the Western chess game that has the same capturing movement as the cannon. It moves in exactly the same way as the rook (including being able to cross the river): it can travel horizontally or vertically to any position on the board. However, it can capture an opponent's piece only if there is one piece (belonging to either side) between it and the piece to be captured. In other words, the cannon jumps over one piece to capture the opponent's piece, like a cannon-ball being fired and destroying the opponent upon landing. If the cannon does not intend to capture a piece, it cannot make this jumping move.

⦿ 馬 **Knight** (N) *ma,* horse

The movement of the knight, like that of the knight of West-

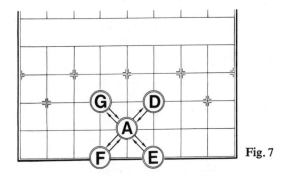

Fig. 7

ern chess, can be thought of as an L-shaped movement. For example, the knight in the position shown in Figure 6 can go to any of the eight positions A, B, V, D, E, F, G, or H in the next move (it can cross the river). But there is an obstacle that can block the legs of the horse. If there is a piece (belonging to either side) in position X, the knight is not allowed to move to either B or V, but it can move to any of the positions D, E, F, G, H, or A. Similarly, suppose there are pieces in positions X and Y, but not in positions W and Z. The knight can then move to A, H, G, or F; however, positions B and V are blocked by the piece in position X, and positions D and E by the piece in position Y. In the worst case, if there are pieces in positions W, X, Y, and Z, the knight cannot move anywhere.

🏵 士 (仕) **Counsellor** (S) *shi,* counsellor

The counsellor can only move along the diagonal lines between the five positions A, D, E, F, and G inside the palace, and may only move one space at a time (Fig. 7). At the start of the game, the two counsellors are placed in positions E and F. From these positions (and from positions G and D) a counsellor can go to position A in the next move. If a counsellor is in position A, it can move to positions D, E, F, or G.

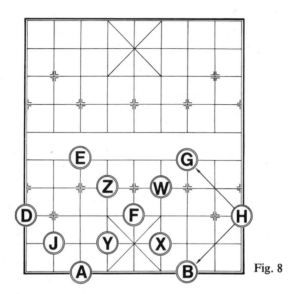

Fig. 8

🐘 象 (blue) **Minister** (M) *xiang,* elephant
🔴 相 (red) **Minister** (M) *xiang,* minister

The minister cannot cross the river. At the beginning of the game, the two ministers are in positions A and B (Fig. 8). The ministers move only in a diagonal direction and exactly two diagonal spaces at a time. For example, from position A a minister can move to D or F; from position H it can move to G or B; and if it is in F, it can go to E, G, B, or A.

As in the case of the knight, there is an obstacle that can block the legs of the elephant (or minister). When there is a piece (belonging to either side) one diagonal space from the minister, the minister is not allowed to move beyond that piece. For example, if a minister is in position F and there are pieces in positions Z and X, the minister cannot move to E or B.

㊨ 卒 (blue) **Pawn (P)** *zu*, foot soldier

㊝ 兵 (red) **Pawn (P)** *bing*, foot soldier

A pawn may move only one space at a time. Before crossing the river, it may move forward vertically, but it is not allowed to move horizontally. After crossing the river it can move either horizontally or vertically. A pawn may not move diagonally or backward. Therefore, when a pawn reaches the far line of the opposite side, it can only move back and forth horizontally one space at a time. Unlike in Western chess, the pawn is not promoted when it reaches the far line. As with the other pieces, it can capture any piece of the opponent's occupying the positions to which it may move.

2 · RULES OF PLAY

There are few strict rules in Chinese chess. Nevertheless, along with the standard rules, some informal restrictions to resolve the ambiguities that may arise are suggested.

1. Red usually makes the first move. Each player makes one move at a time.

2. Each player should make a move within a specified period of time.

3. The game should be played on a touch-move policy: whenever a player touches a piece, that piece must be moved next.

4. Check: When a player moves into a position which puts the opponent's king in check, that is, when the opponent's king could be captured in the next move, the player should call "check."

5. A player cannot check perpetually; specifically, a player may not, with the same piece, put the opponent in check more than three times in a row without either side moving any other pieces. For example, in Figure 9, red has just put blue's king in check. It is illegal for the red rook to keep chasing blue's king back and forth on lines 4, 5, and 6.

6. Checkmate: When a player puts the opponent's king in check, and the opponent cannot move the king out of check and cannot block the check with another piece, the first player wins.

7. Stalemate: When a player cannot make a legal move with any remaining pieces, the player is "stalemated." In Chinese chess, a stalemate is a loss (not a draw, as in Western chess). For example, in Figure 10 blue's king cannot move, since it would only move into check due to the position of red's knight. Blue's cannon also cannot move. Therefore, blue loses.

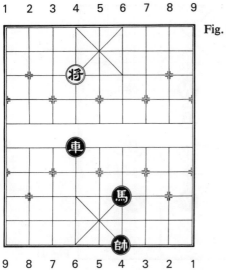

Fig. 9

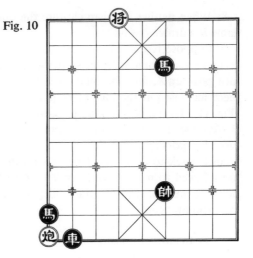

Fig. 10

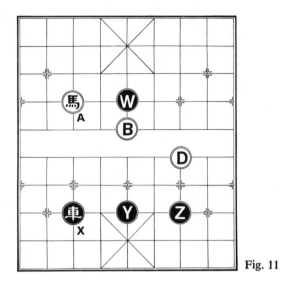

Fig. 11

8. When neither side can capture the opponent's king, the game is a draw.

9. Suppose red uses a certain piece to attempt to capture a certain piece of blue's. At the start, the red piece has just moved into position X, and the blue piece is in position A; the red piece has just put the blue piece in danger of being captured (Fig. 11). To escape, the blue piece moves to another position, B. Assume that the red piece follows up and chases the blue piece by moving to position Y. Now, if the blue piece moves from B back to A to avoid being captured, the red piece is not allowed to move back from Y to X to chase the blue. To be more precise, such chasing is illegal when three conditions exist simultaneously:

(a) In either of positions A or B, the blue piece is not protected (that is, if the blue piece is captured by the red piece in either of these positions, then no other piece of blue's can capture the red piece in return)

(b) Blue uses exactly two positions, A and B, to avoid being captured by red

(c) Red uses exactly two positions, X and Y, to chase after blue

Note that if any one of these conditions are violated, continual chasing is allowed. Specifically,

(a) if the blue piece is protected in either A or B, then the red piece is allowed to chase after blue continually;

(b) if the blue piece uses more than two different positions to avoid being captured (e.g., positions A, B, *and* D), the red piece is allowed to follow up and continue to chase using any positions (e.g., position Z);

(c) if the red piece uses more than two positions to chase after the blue piece, then the red piece is allowed to continue chasing no matter where blue moves (e.g., if blue moves to B and back to A, red may move to Y and then to W to chase blue).

3 · VALUES AND USES OF THE PIECES

It is difficult to give a precise ranking to the chess pieces. However, they can roughly be valued as follows:

Piece	Value
Rook	9
Cannon	4.5
Knight	4
Counsellor	2
Minister	2
Pawn (after crossing the river)	2
Pawn (before crossing the river)	1

The king, of course, is the most valuable piece, but cannot really be ranked in the same way as the rest.

The following brief analysis helps to reflect the defensive and offensive capabilities of the pieces, although these will become clearer as you actually start playing the game.

King 帥, 将

At the beginning of the game, the king is often not able to exercise its offensive power. Although the king is the soul of the game, it tends to weaken its own kingdom by extracting pieces for its protection. However, when the number of pieces on the board decreases, it is often found that the king plays a vital role in setting up a winning strategy.

Rook 車

There is a saying that "One who does not move the rook within the first three moves is not a good player." Another proverb says, "One rook can make ten pieces shiver." Generally speaking, at the beginning of the game a rook has a value of no less than that of a cannon and knight combined. The power of a rook decreases only slightly when the game approaches the middle stages. During the end-game, however, a rook can usually not penetrate the opponent's defense alone. For example, a single rook cannot destroy a well-coordinated defense set up by two counsellors and two ministers (see Fig. 31, p. 66), but a knight and a cannon together (without a rook) can win in such a situation (see Fig. 64, p. 87). With the help of other pieces, though, the power of a rook at the end-game can be magnified enormously.

Cannon 炮

The swift movement of a cannon makes it an important piece in both defense and offense. It can destroy a solid defense from a distance. Between the opening and the mid-game, it is perhaps not wise to lose a cannon in exchange for a knight.

On the other hand, it is said that a cannon is less useful than a knight in end-games. This is because there are usually very few pieces at this stage, so the cannon's capturing power is greatly reduced, whereas a knight has less chance of being blocked. However, this generalization should not be adopted as an absolute principle. For example, a defense set up by a cannon together with two ministers and two counsellors cannot be destroyed by an opponent's rook-pawn pair (see Fig. 43, p. 72); but if the cannon is replaced by a knight, the rook-pawn pair always wins (see Fig. 40, p.70). There is thus no strict rule that can be stated as to whether a cannon or a knight is more valuable. It depends very much on the situation.

Knight 馬

It is not easy to move the two knights smoothly and efficiently, and it is said that one who can use the knights effectively is at least a "second class" player. In the opening, the knights are often responsible for protecting the pawns. In the mid-game, the knights are useful pioneers in attacking.

Counsellor 士

The prime responsibility of the counsellors is to protect the king. Losing one of the counsellors can greatly endanger the king's safety.

Minister 相, 象

If it can be said that the counsellors constitute the king's inner protective layer, then it is the ministers who act as the outer protective layer. It is very difficult to judge whether the counsellors or the ministers are better guards. For example, losing one counsellor makes the king easily vulnerable to two rooks, and losing one minister makes the king easily vulnerable to a cannon.

Pawn 兵, 卒

In the early stages of the game, the pawns are mainly used to block the enemy. The pawns have various functions according to their positions. For example, the pawn on line 5 is an extremely important defender for the central territory. Those on lines 3 and 7 usually help to obstruct attacks. The invasions from the left and right sides are blocked by the pawns on lines 9 and 1, respectively. Very often, the pawns are used as bridges by the cannons to exert pressure on the opposite side.

In the end-game, it is not uncommon that one extra pawn can lead to victory. The position of a pawn in the end-game— whether it has gone beyond a certain horizontal line or beyond the opponent's king—often determines the outcome of the game. A pawn's moving too far can ruin that player's chances of winning (see Fig. 60, p. 84; Fig. 86, p. 102).

4 · NOTATION

The abbreviations K, R, N, C, S, M, and P for king, rook, knight, cannon, counsellor, minister, and pawn, respectively, together with numbers and other symbols, are used to record the moves of the game. Basically, a piece has three modes of movement: forward (denoted in the notation by "f"), backward "b," and horizontal "h." The frame of reference is always the vertical-line numbering system (1 to 9, right to left) of the side to which that piece belongs. A few examples will make this system of notation clear. Refer to Figure 12.

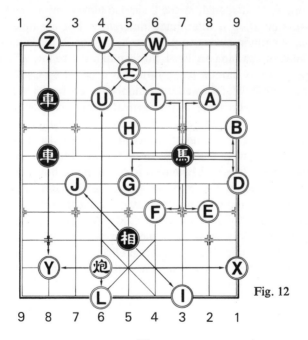

Fig. 12

First, let us examine a piece which can move vertically, the blue cannon 炮 on line 4. The notation for the movement of this piece to position U is C4b6, or "cannon on line 4, back 6 spaces." If the cannon moves instead to position L, the notation is C4f1, or "cannon on line 4, forward 1 space." Thus, if a piece moves vertically, the notation shows the name of the piece, the line it is on, the direction it moves "f" or "b," and the number of spaces it moves. Put another way, if a piece *can* move vertically, the symbols "f" or "b" followed by a number always mean vertical movement that number of spaces. (For pieces which cannot move vertically, "f" or "b" plus a number have a different meaning, discussed below.)

For any other direction of movement besides the vertical—horizontal, diagonal, or the L-shaped movement of the knight—the notation is interpreted differently. For example, if the line-4 cannon moves to position X, on line 9, the notation is C4h9, or "cannon on line 4, horizontal move to line 9." Movement of this cannon to position Y is denoted by C4h2. Thus, the symbol "h" followed by a number refers to the horizontal movement of a piece to the *vertical line* of that number.

The ministers and counsellors move diagonally. When the red minister 相, on line 5, moves to position J, which is on line 7, the move is denoted by M5f7, or "minister on line 5, forward to line 7." Movement to position I is shown by M5b3, or "minister on line 5, backward to line 3." (Remember that the minister moves exactly two diagonal spaces.) Note here that the "f" and "b" plus a number used with a piece which cannot move vertically mean movement to the vertical line of that number. (Compare the discussion of the notation of the moves of the cannon, above.) Similarly, the four possible moves of the blue counsellor 士, on line 5, are

to T: S5f6	to V: S5b4
to U: S5f4	to W: S5b6

The notation for moves of the knight uses "f" and "b" in the same way as that of the minister and cannon. The movement of the red knight 馬, on line 3, to position A is denoted by N3f2, or "knight on line 3, forward to line 2." The other possible moves for this knight are

to B: N3f1	to G: N3b5
to D: N3b1	to H: N3f5
to E: N3b2	to T: N3f4
to F: N3b4	

When two pieces of the same kind belonging to the same player are on the same line, an additional notational convention is observed: the pieces are distinguished by calling them "f" and "r," for front and rear, respectively, and the vertical line number on which the piece rests is not named. For example, there are two red rooks 車 on line 8. The front rook is the one toward the top of the diagram. If this rook moves to position Z, the notation is fRf2, or "front rook, forward 2 spaces." The rear rook moving to position Y is denoted by rRb4, or "rear rook, backward 4 spaces."

The following chart summarizes the notation as it relates to the movement capabilities of each of the pieces.

PIECE	MOVEMENT SYMBOL	INTERPRETATION
K, R, C, P	h (horizontal)	Horizontal movement to the *vertical line number* stated
	f (forward) b (backward)	Vertical movement the stated *number of lines*
M, S	f, b	Diagonal movement to the *vertical line number* stated
N	f, b	L-shaped movement to the *vertical line number* stated

Long lists of moves are given in the standard double-column format. Red's moves are always on the left. An example, taken from the middle of a game, follows. (The arrows, shown only in this example, give the sequence of moves.)

	Red	Blue			Red	Blue
	C5h4 ⟶	C3f8	**b.**			R3f2
	K5f1 ⟵	C3h1*[a]			P3f1	C8h9
	C7f2	R1h3			N3f2	R8f3
	C7h5*[b]	R3f8			(etc.)	
	K5b1	R3b3				
	(etc.)					
a.	C7f3	R1h3				
	C7h5	R3f8				
	(etc.)					

An asterisk with a lower case letter or letters indicates a variation. In the above chart, after blue makes move C3h1, the game can either continue with the set of moves in the section marked "a," or with the moves under C3h1 (i.e., C7f2, R1h3, etc.) in the main chart. Similarly, after red makes move C7h5 in the main chart, the game can continue with the set of moves in the section marked "b," or with the moves following C7h5 (i.e., R3f8, K5b1, R3b3, etc.) in the main chart.

PART · 2 · PLAYING THE GAME

5 · OPENING OF THE GAME

The opening is the foundation of the whole game, and the choice of opening move directly influences the subsequent development of the game. In this chapter, eight different opening strategies for the lead move (for the player who makes the first move in the game) and another eight strategies for the response move are given. Red is assumed to be the lead player in all the following examples. It will be helpful, if not essential, from this point on to actually have a chessboard and pieces to use along with the text.

Note that many series of moves can be started on either the left or the right side of the board. For example, the opening moves C2h5 and C8h5 are equivalent. However, to avoid repetition, only the series of moves starting with, say, C2h5 is given in most of the examples below. The player can infer and use the equivalent series beginning with C8h5.

LEAD MOVES

Central Cannon

The Central Cannon opening is the most common lead move. It starts with C2h5 or C8h5 and has the effect of threatening the opponent's central pawn directly. This move also opens itself to four common subsequent arrangements described immediately below. (Other important variations on the Central Cannon are discussed separately under Five-Six Cannon, Five-Seven Cannon, and Five-Eight Cannon, below.)

1. CENTRAL PAWN ADVANCE/CHAINED KNIGHTS: Red's successive moves are C2h5, N8f7, N2f3, P5f1, N7f5, P5f1 (or C8h5, N8f7, N2f3, P5f1, N3f5, P5f1). This series of moves will allow red to choose to attack line 3, 4, 5, 6, or 7—whichever is

the weakest—by advancing the pair of knights (hence called "chained knights") escorted by either a horizontal rook, R1h2 (or R9h8, if the first move was C8h5), or a vertical rook, R1f1 (or R9f1). The main goal is to attack the opponent's central line.

2. RIVER-GUARDING ROOK: Red's successive moves are C2h5, N2f3, R1h2, R2f4. The purpose is to bring together two rooks, two cannons, and one knight to attack the opponent's right side.

3. RIVER-GUARDING CANNON: Red's successive moves are C2h5, N2f3, R1h2, N8f7, P7f1, C8f2. This opening can be used only if blue also moves P7f1 within these first six moves. The purpose is for red to make P3f1 in the next move and take blue's line-7 pawn in exchange for red's line-3 pawn. This will clear paths for the knights and the line-9 rook. The attack tends to concentrate on the opponent's left side.

4. LINE-7 PAWN ADVANCE: The successive moves are the same as those of the River-Guarding Cannon, except that C8f2 is replaced by N7f6. The knight is used as the pioneer for the attack, which tends to concentrate on the opponent's right side. The attack can also be shifted to the opponent's left side by moving R2f6 and R2h3 subsequently.

Five-Six Cannon

Red's moves C2h5 and C8h6 give the Five-Six Cannon opening, one which is readily adapted to both offense and defense. The main purpose of using this opening is to counteract the Screening Knights response (namely, blue's moves N2f3 and N8f7; see p. 40). The two moves need not be the first two moves of the game, nor must they necessarily be made consecutively. They may be made when it is apparent that the opponent is using the Screening Knights response.

Five-Seven Cannon

In the Five-Seven Cannon opening, red's successive moves are C2h5, N2f3, R1h2, N8f9, C8h7. The main purpose here is to counteract a Screening Knights response. The line-7 cannon is used to threaten the opponent's line-3 knight.

Five-Eight Cannon

Sometimes called the Central and Cross-River Cannon or the Central Cannon/Line-3 Pawn Advance, the Five-Eight Cannon opening begins with C2h5 and C8f4. Red continues with N2f3, R1h2, P3f1. This opening can be used only if the opponent has also moved P3f1 within these first five moves. The line-8 cannon has two possible functions. First, the move C8h7 can block the opponent's line-3 knight (assuming this knight has moved out) and aim at capturing the line-3 minister. Second, the move C8h3 can block the opponent's line-7 knight (again, if this knight has moved out) and aim at capturing the line-7 minister. Either of these two moves can escort the line-3 knight and line-3 pawn across the river. This opening is mainly used to counterattack the Screening Knights response.

Three-Step Tiger

Red's first three successive moves N2f3, C2h1, R1h2 make up the Three-Step Tiger opening. This opening can be switched to the Screening Knights response, the Cross-Palace Knights response (see p. 42), and some other openings. The particular feature of this opening is that the rook is rushed out.

Predicting Prophet

The Predicting Prophet opens with either P3f1 or P7f1. Its purpose is to make an outlet for the line-3 or line-7 knight and at the same time to detect the opponent's opening strategy.

This opening can be switched to many other openings, including the Central Cannon and the Screening Knights response. Consequently, if red starts with the Predicting Prophet, blue cannot tell how red will "really" open. In order to use this opening effectively, one has to be very experienced, as well as to be ready to perform well in the mid-game.

Cross-Palace Cannon

The Cross-Palace Cannon opens with C2h6, N2f3, R1h2, R2f6. Red continues with S4f5 and M7f5 so that a solid defense is set up. This opening has the disadvantage of forcing the pieces to be squeezed into the lower left-hand corner.

Central Double Cannon

Red's three moves C2h5, C5b1, C8h5 make up the Central Double Cannon opening. Red's subsequent moves are N2f3, P5f1, N3f5, P5f1. The two cannons here have tremendous power in bombing the opponent's central line. However, the opener's own defense is weak and vulnerable to numerous attacks.

The above eight examples are the most common openings. They can be modified to different variations, many of which will become clear as the reader begins playing.

RESPONSE MOVES

Screening Knights

It has been said that the Screening Knights response can always destroy a Central Cannon opening. Although this is not absolutely correct, it is the most common strategy used to react to the Central Cannon, providing a very solid defense and preparing the player to set out for attack.

The moves which make up the Screening Knights response are N2f3 and N8f7; they need not be made at the very beginning of the game, nor in direct consecutive order. There are several important things to remember when this opening is used: (1) the line-3 and/or line-7 pawns must be advanced in time so that the knights are not blocked, (2) the cannons should guard or cross the river and thus help in the offense and defense, (3) each rook-knight-cannon trio must communicate properly.

Lee Cannon

If the leading move C2h5 (or C8h5) is responded to by C8h5 (or C2h5), two central cannons from the same side of the board will be facing each other. This response is called the Lee Cannon. Both players are in threatening positions.

Adverse Cannon

If the leading move C2h5 is responded to by C2h5 (or C8h5 by C8h5), two central cannons from opposite sides of the board will be facing each other. This response is called the Adverse Cannon. Each of the two players will concentrate pieces for attack in different parts of the board. As a response opening, the Adverse Cannon is relatively less flexible than the Lee Cannon and so is less commonly used.

Lame Knight

Blue's two response moves N2f3 and N8f9 give the Lame Knight response. The subsequent moves are usually R9h8, M3f5, S6f5. The major disadvantage of this opening is that the central pawn is only protected by one knight and is thus easily captured. Furthermore, the two knights cannot move freely. The success of this strategy depends very much on what the player does in the mid-game and end-game.

Side-Cannon Screen

Blue's successive moves in the Side-Cannon Screen response are N2f3, C8h6, N8f7. This response has potential as a defense against a Central Cannon attack. A disadvantage is that it is difficult to utilize the line-9 rook fully.

Cross-Palace Knights

Blue's successive moves in the Cross-Palace Knights response are M3f5, N2f4, N4f6 ("moving across the palace"). Because the knights are not well protected, this series of moves is not very effective in defending against a Central Cannon opening. However, it has definite potential in resisting the Screening Knights and Lame Knight openings.

Pawn vs. Pawn

The leading move P3f1 responded to by P3f1 gives a Pawn *vs.* Pawn opening. This response can be switched to either the Screening Knights or the Cross-Palace Knights openings. This strategy is not as aggressive as other openings.

Cannon Response Openings

In responding to the Central Cannon, there are three rare Cannon Response openings. The disadvantage with these is that the pieces tend to cluster in one corner and are thus not very flexible in adapting to different attacks.

1. LEFT DOUBLE CANNON: Blue's two moves C8f1 and C2h8 set up a double cannon arrangement on line 8. This protects the central pawn and at the same time blocks the opponent's rook from moving R1h2.

2. PARROT CANNON: The opening moves for red and blue, respectively, are as follows:

Red	Blue
C2h5	N8f7
N2f3	R9f1
R1h2	C8b1

Blue can then move its line-8 cannon C8h5 (if red attacks line 5); C8h1 (to concentrate the attack on red's left side); C8h2 (to set up a Right Double Cannon on line 2, blocking red's rook from moving R9h8); or C8h3 (if red uses its line-7 knight —assuming that N8f7 was previously made—as the attacking pioneer, then the next move, P3f1, will block the knight).

3. DRAKE-AND-DUCK CANNON: The opening moves are as follows:

Red	Blue
C2h5	N2f3
N2f3	P7f1
R1h2	R9f2
N8f7	C2b1

In the next step, blue's cannon on line 2 can either move C2h8 (to chase the rook) or C2h7 (to attack red's line-3 pawn).

Although the terms "lead move" and "response move" indicate that they are generally used by the lead and responding player (red and blue), respectively, this need not always be the case. The responder can attempt to force a lead-move strategy against the lead player, in which case the lead player might have to use a response move.

6 · THE MID-GAME

Roughly speaking, the mid-game starts when each player has made about ten moves after the opening. While there is, of course, no one formula for playing well in the mid-game, some informal general principles are stated here. Following these, example sets of moves will demonstrate two important mid-game strategies, "sacrifice" and "countersacrifice." The reader is also referred to Chapter 8, in which artificially made up mid-game arrangements are presented in the form of exercises.

Guidelines for the Mid-Game

1. Build up a solid defense before considering an attack or capturing the opponent's pieces.

2. Do not capture a "dead piece" (one which cannot be saved easily and can be captured within the next several moves) in a hurry, or be greedy about sacrificial pieces.

3. Do not attack without enough reinforcement.

4. Break the opponent's left-to-right communication so that his pieces are isolated and strength dispersed.

5. Capturing at least one minister and/or one counsellor will greatly undermine the opponent's defense.

6. Use a rook to block the opponent's knight from crossing the river, and capture the knights with the help of cannons and knights.

7. Limit the range of movement of an opponent's rook by blocking it with a protected knight or cannon.

8. If an opponent's cannon is protecting some other pieces, try to take that cannon in an exchange or to force it to move elsewhere.

9. Use at least two pieces to attack the opponent's central line, left side, or right side, whichever is the weakest.

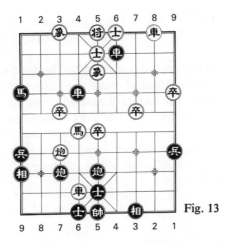

Fig. 13

10. Exchange the opponent's significant pieces and attack the weakly protected pieces.

11. If the opponent's pieces are concentrated on one side, then gather enough pieces for protection on that side.

12. If your piece is under attack, it is more advantageous to attack a piece of the opponent's than to try to escape or protect your piece.

Sacrifice and Countersacrifice

Throughout the mid-game, it is important to watch out for any opportunity that can lead to overall control. Consider the example set-up shown in Figure 13. Red has one extra piece, a cannon. But there is a danger on the red side: the two ministers are not chained together. ("Chained together" means that two pieces are one move away from each other's positions. For example, the two blue ministers in Figure 13 are chained together.) It is now blue's turn to move. If blue moves R8f9

K帥(将) · R車 · N馬 · C炮 · S士 · M相(象) · P兵(卒) · **45**

and uses its two rooks, its knight, its cannon, and its central pawn to attack, the red player will find it difficult to defend its king.

Now suppose blue does move R8f9. There are six ways that red may respond. None of these ways can rescue red; blue can always win. The six sets of moves are shown below. (The designation "win" at the end of a list of moves means that all the steps to the win are shown; "will win" means that not all the moves to the final win are shown, but that the game obviously leads to a win for the player in whose column the designation appears.)

	Red	Blue		Red	Blue
1.		R8f9	2.		R8f9
	K5h4	R8h7		S5b4	C3h5
	K4f1	N4f5		S6f5	R8h7
	R6b5	N5b7*a		R4b7	R4h2
	K4f1	R7b1		C7h6	R2f1
	S5f6	R7b1		C6b2	N4f5
	K4b1	R7h4		R6b4	N5b7
	K4b1	R4f1		S5f4	N7f6
	K4h5	N7f5			(will win)
	S4f5	C3h5			
	K5h4	R4h5	3.		R8f9
	R4b6	R5f1		C5h4	R8h7
	K4f1	R5h6		C4b2	C3h5*a
		(win)		S5f6	N4f5
				S6f5	N5f7
a.	C7h3	R7b2			(win)
	S5f6	R7f1			
	K4f1	C3f1	a.	C7h5	N4f5
		(will win)		R6b5	N5f7
					(win)

	Red	Blue			Red	Blue
4.		R8f9		**6.**		R8f9
	N9f8	R8h7*a			C5f5	M3f5
	S5b4	C3h5			N9f8	R8h7
	C5f2	N4f5			S5b4	C3h4
	S6f5	N5f7			R6h9	N4f2*a
		(win)			R9f3	C4b6
					N8f6	S5b4
a.	R4b8	N4f5				(will win)
	R4h3	R4b5				
		(will win)		**a.**	R9h6	P5h4
					R6h9	R4f1
5.		R8f9			K5f1	R7b1
	R4b5	R8h7			R4b7	N2f4
	S5b4	C3h5				(will win)
	R4h5	P5f1				
	C5f5	M3f5				
	S6f5	P5f1				
	S5b6	R4h6				
		(will win)				

If blue does not realize the fatal **R8f9** move, but makes **C3h4** instead (to chase the red rook), red will have a chance to win. The key to red's winning is for red to let its rook be sacrificed. The successive moves are as follows:

	Red	Blue				Red	Blue
7.		C3h4	*or*	**8.**			C3h4
	C7f7	C4b3				C7f7	M5b3
	C5f5	S5f4				R6b2	etc.
	N9f8					(red has gained control)

Continuing with series 7, blue has only two choices: **R8f9** or **N4b3**. The successive moves for each of these choices are as follows (there are a total of two sets of moves following R8f9 and four sets of moves following N4b3):

	Red	Blue		Red	Blue
a(i).		R8f9	**b(ii).**		N4b3
	C5h3	S6f5		N8b6	K5h4
	C3f2	S5f6		N6f8	N3b2
	N8b6	K5h4		C5h9	
	N6f8	K4h5		(will win)	
	R4h6				
	(will win)		**b(iii).**		N4b3
				N8b6	K5h4
a(ii).		R8f9		N6f8	K4h5
	C5h3	C4h7		C5h6	N3b2
	C3f2	S6f5		C6h9	
	R4f1	K5h6		(will win)	
	N8f6				
	(win)		**b(iv).**		N4b3
				N8b6	N3b4
b(i).		N4b3		N6f8	R8f9
	N8b6	N3b4		C5h3	N4f2
	N6f8	R8f9		C3h6	R8h7
	C5h3	N4f2		S5b4	R4f1
	K5h4	S6f5		K5h6	P5h4
	C3h5	S5f6			(win)
	C5h6	R8h7			
	K4f1	N2b4			
	N8f6				
	(win)				

In the above cases, except for b(iv), red won mainly for two reasons: (1) because blue did not move R8f9 in the first place, but moved C3h4; and (2) because red sacrificed its line-6 rook. If, after blue moved C3h4 (the first move of series 7), red had

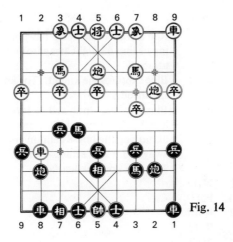

Fig. 14

moved R6h8, that is, had *not* let its rook be sacrificed, red might not have been able to win after all.

In Figure 14, a tactic similar to sacrifice, called counter-sacrifice, is demonstrated. It is now red's move. Many people would make P7f1, but we shall discuss C2f1 instead. The successive moves are listed below, with commentary.

	Red	*Blue*	
1.	C2f1		Red's purpose here is to invite the blue rook on line 2 to move R2h4 so that red can sacrifice its line-6 knight, move P3f1, and attempt to gain overall control.
2.		R2h4	Blue realizes that red is trying to allow this knight to be sacrificed. Blue goes along with this, but is at the same time preparing to make a countersacrifice.

	Red	Blue
3.	P3f1		Red advances its line-3 pawn instead of moving its line-6 knight away from the blue rook's attack.
4.		R4b1	Blue captures the knight. (The knight has been sacrificed.)
5.	P3f1	P5f1	Blue realizes that red is trying to push its line-3 pawn forward. Blue moves P5f1 instead of moving the line-8 cannon and line-7 knight away from the attack of red's line-3 pawn. This is a countersacrifice.
6.	P3f1	N7f5	
	P3h4	P5f1	
	C8f2	R4b1	
	P5f1	R4f2	
	P4h5	N3f5	
	C2h5	N5f7	
	R1h2	R9h8	
	C8b1	P3f1	
	P7f1	N7f6	At this point, blue is in control.

The significance of blue's countersacrifice is as follows: Blue realized early that red wanted to sacrifice its knight—which might ultimately have been advantageous for red—but blue knew that it could counter with its own sacrifice (the "countersacrifice" in step 5) shortly, so it let red make the sacrifice. Thus, while a sacrifice alone may be important in gaining control, being able to envision a countersacrifice is certainly to one's advantage.

As a final example of the use of a sacrifice move, the complete sets of moves for a Central Cannon/River-Guarding Rook opening against a Screening Knights response is given. In the mid-game, blue sacrifices a Knight, the most crucial part of the whole scheme. Many players have concluded that once the

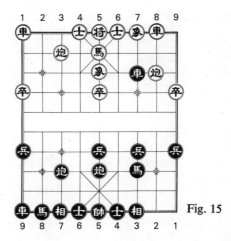

Fig. 15

sacrificial knight is captured by red, blue will gain control no matter how red moves. (The designation "controls" below the list of moves refers to a stage earlier than a clear "will win" situation.)

As usual, red moves first:

Red	Blue		Red	Blue
C2h5	N8f7		R2h7	C2b1
N2f3	R9h8		C8h7	C2h3
R1h2	P3f1		R7h3	P7f1
R2f4	N2f3		R3f1	M3f5
P7f1	P3f1		R3f2	N3b5

The arrangement should now be that shown in Figure 15.

Red	Blue		Red	Blue
C5f4*a	C3f8		C7f2	R1h3*e
K5f1	C3h1*b		C7h5*h	R3f8*i,1

K 帥 (将) · R 車 · N 馬 · C 炮 · S 士 · M 相 (象) · P 兵 (卒) · **51**

Red	Blue		Red	Blue
K5b1	R3b3*m,n,o	**c.**	N3f5	R8f3
P3f1*p	C8f7*b',c'		R3h5	R3h5
N3f4	R3h4		P5f1	M7f5
R3h5	R4h5			(controls)
P5f1	M7f5			
P5f1	R8f3	**d.**	N3f5	R3h4
P3f1	R8h5		N5b7	R8h3
P5f1	N5f3			(will win)
P5f1	N3f2			
	(controls)	**e.**	C7h2	C8h9
			C2h3	R3f3
a.			R3b1	R3h5
	C3f1		R3h5	R8f8*f
R3b1	C3f7		K5b1	R8h2
K5f1	C3h1		C3h5	R2f1*g
R3h2	R1h3		K5f1	R2b1
P3f1	R8f1		K5f1	R2b1
N3f4	R8h6		K5b1	R2h7
N4f6	R6f3		K5h6	R7h2
C7h3	C8h7		R5h6	R2f1
N6f5	M7f5		K6f1	R2b8
C3f5			P3f1	C1h2
(will win)			P3f1	C2b7
			P3f1	C2h4
b.	C7f3 R1h3		K6h5	R2f6
C7f3	R1h3			(will win)
C7h5	R3f8			
K5b1	R3b4	**f.**	K5f1	N5f3
P5f1	C8f7*c		R5h6	N3f2
R3b1	R8f8*d		R6b3	R8h2
N3b2	R3f5		N8f6	C1b1
S4f5	R3h2			(will win)
rCh7	R2h3			
C7h8	C1h2	**g.**	R5h7	C9h7
S5f6	R8f1		N3b5	R2b3
	(will win)			

Red	Blue		Red	Blue
R7b6	R3h5		K4h5	R3h2
	(will win)		rCh7	R6h3
			C7h6	R2f1
h.	R3f2		R3h4	C4b3
P3f1	C8h9		S4f5	R3b1
N3f2	R8f3		S5f6	R2h5
C5h3			K5h4	R5h6
(controls)			K4h5	R6b7
				(will win)
i.	K5f1	C8f5		
N3b5	C1b2*j	**n.**	M3f5	R3h2
K5h6	C8f1*k		rCh7	R2b5
N5f4	R8f7		P3f1	C8f7
M3f5	R3b5		N3b2	R8f3
	(will win)		C5b2	R8h5
			R3h4	N5f3
j.	K5h4	R3b1		(will win)
K4b1	C8h6			
	(will win)	**o.**	S4f5	C8f4
			P3f1	R8f3
k.	N5f6	C8h6		C5b1	R3h2
	(will win)		R3h4	R2f4
			K5h4	R8h6
l.	N8f6	C8h9		R4b1	R2b6
K5h4	R3b1		K4f1	R2h6
	(will win)		S5f4	R6f1
			C5f1	R6h5
m.	K5f1	C8f7		(will win)
K5h4	R8f8			
K4f1	R8h7	**p.**		C8f4*q,s
N3b1	C1b2		M3f5*u	R3h2
N8f9	R3f2		rCh7	R2b5*w
M3f5	C8h4		N3f4*x	C8f3*y
N9b8	R3f1		M5b3	C8b4
M5b3	R7h6		R3f2*z	R8f4*a'

	Red	Blue
	N4f3	C8h3
	N3f5	C3f4
	S6f5	C3b5
	N8f7	R2f9
	S5b6	C3h5
	M3f5	R2b6
	S6f5	C5b2
		(will win)
q.	N3f4*r	R3h5
	P5f1	C8h5
	R3b1	R8f6
		(controls)
r.		C8b1
	rCf3	M7f5
	N4f6	C8b1
	N6f5	C8h5
	M3f5	C5b2
	M5f7	R8f6
	R3h5	R8h5
	S4f5	R5b2
	P3f1	R5h7
	C5b4	R7h2
	R5b4	
	(controls)	
s.	S4f5	R8f3
	C5b1	R3h2
	R3f2	R8b1*t
	S5f4	C8f3
	N3b2	R2f4
	R3b4	R2b7
	S6f5	R8f7
	K5h6	R8h7

	Red	Blue
	K6f1	R7h3
	fCh8	R2h4
	S5f6	R3b1
	K6b1	R4f5
	K6h5	R4h2
		(will win)
t.	M3f5	R2f4
	R3b4	C8b2
		(will win)
u.		R3h4
	S4f5*v	C8h1
	R3h4	R8f6
	R4f1	R4b3
	P3f1	C1h3
	S5f6	
(neither side has control yet)		
v.		R8f3
	C5b1	R8f1
	P3f1	
	(controls)	
w.	N3f2	R8f5
	C7h2	R2f9
	R3b1	R2b5
	M5b7	R2h8
	C5b2	C8h1
		(controls)
x.		C8b1
	R3f2	R8f2
	C7f3	
	(controls)	

	Red	Blue			Red	Blue
y.	S4f5	C8b4		c'.	P3f1	R3h2
	R3f2				R3h5	R2h5
	(controls)				P5f1	M7f5
					P5f1	R8f6
z.		R8h7			N3f4	R8h7
	N4f6	R7f2			P3h2	C8b4
	N6f8				K5f1	R7h6*d'
	(will win)				N4f3	C8h5
					P5h6	R6b3
a'.	P3f1	C8h3			N3f1	C5h2
	P3h2	R2f9			P6f1	C2b3
		(will win)			N1f3	R6b2
					N3b2	C2f1
b'.	N3b2	R3h2				(controls)
	R3f2	R2h5				
	R3h2	R5f1		d'.	N4f6	C8h5
	S4f5	R5b3			P5h4	C1h4
		(controls)				(will win)

7 · THE END-GAME

In the final stage of the game, the end-game, each player is usually left with only a few pieces. Some experts suggest that it is the end-game that beginners should practice before any other technique. In this chapter, end-game combinations that occur frequently in actual play are presented. Numerous artificially made up end-game exercises are given in Chapter 8; readers are strongly recommended to try those as well.

The various end-games in this chapter are grouped into eighteen categories according to the remaining pieces on one side, here, the red side. The name of the category reflects these remaining pieces. (In certain specific cases, one or two ministers and/or counsellors also remain on the red side; however, such combinations are not assigned separate categories.) The headings for the specific arrangements show red's pieces *vs.* blue's pieces, omitting the kings. It is always red's turn to move. As in Chapter 6, the designations "win" or "will win" are given at the bottom of the appropriate column; additionally, "draw" is stated when further attempts at winning by either of the players are futile.

In many cases the outcome for a given combination of pieces can be predicted with certainty (or virtual certainty) as a win for one side or a draw. In many other cases, the arrangement of pieces as well as their combination must be taken into account. These conditions and other comments are stated for each example.

One Rook
1. R *vs.* N, C (Fig. 16)

If the knight and cannon are well coordinated, as in this example, they can force a draw against the rook.

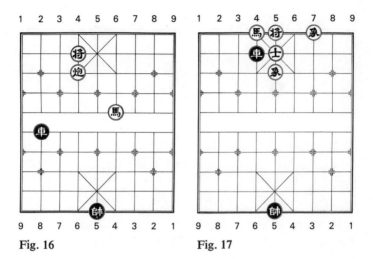

Fig. 16   Fig. 17

Red	Blue
R8h5	N6b4
R5f4	K4b1
R5b2	N4f3
K5h6	K4f1
R5h7	N3b4

Red	Blue
K6h5	K4f5
K5h6	N5b4
K6h5	N4f5
(draw)	

2. R *vs.* N, M, M, S (Fig. 17)

Blue will force a draw if the pieces are arranged in this way by the end-game. Blue can force a draw in other arrangements as well, as long as its pieces are communicating properly.

Red	Blue
K5f1	M7f9
(draw)	

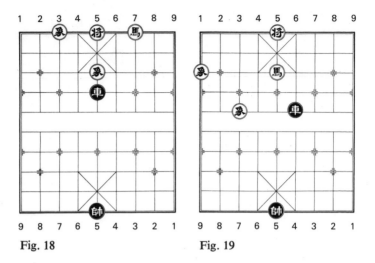

Fig. 18   Fig. 19

3. R *vs*. N, M, M (Figs. 18 and 19)

Generally, one rook can defeat one knight and two ministers. Such a case is shown in Figure 18 (blue cannot force a draw here). An exceptional case is shown in Figure 19, the only arrangement in which blue can force a draw; red cannot win.

(Moves for Fig. 18)

Red	Blue		Red	Blue
R5h4	N7f5		R4b1	N7f8
K5h4	N5f3		K5f1	N8f9
R4f3	K5f1		R4h2	N9b7
K4h5	N3f5		K5b1	K5h6
R4h6	K5h6		R2h4	K6h5
R6b3	N5f7		R4h3	N7b5
R6h4	K6h5		R3b2	
			(will win)	

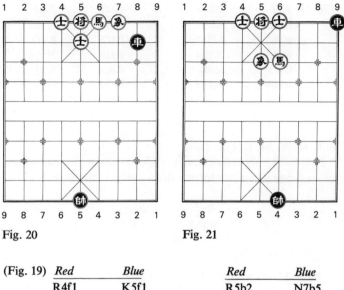

Fig. 20   Fig. 21

(Fig. 19)	*Red*	*Blue*		*Red*	*Blue*
	R4f1	K5f1		R5b2	N7b5
	R4f3	K5h4		K5f1	K4h5
	R4h5	N5f7		(draw)	
	R5b1	K4b1			

4. R *vs*. N, M, S, S (Figs. 20 and 21)

If blue's pieces are communicating well, as in Figure 20, then blue will always be able to force a draw against the rook. On the other hand, if blue's pieces are not communicating properly, as in Figure 21, then the rook will have a chance to win. (It is not impossible for blue to force a draw in this latter case; however, the moves show the way to a red win.)

(Fig. 20)	*Red*	*Blue*
	K5f1	M7f5
	(draw)	

K 帥 (将)・R 車・N 馬・C 炮・S 士・M 相 (象)・P 兵 (卒)・**59**

(Fig. 21) Red	Blue	Red	Blue
K4h5	S4f5	R6h8	K5h4
R1b3	M5f7	R8f2	K4f1
R1h9	K5h4	R8b4	N5b6
R9f3	K4f1	R8h6	S5f4
R9b4	K4b1	K5h6	S6f5
R9h6	K4h5	R6h9	
R6f2	N6f5	(will win)	

5. R *vs.* N, M, P (Fig. 22)

This is the only arrangement in which one knight, one minister, and one pawn can force a draw against one rook.

Red	Blue
R1h5	K5b1
(draw)	

6. R, S, M *vs.* N, S, S, P (Figs. 23 and 24)

Figure 23 shows the only arrangement in which blue can force a draw; note that the blue pawn must be on the second line on the opposite side of the river. An arrangement in which red can win with the same combination of pieces is shown in Figure 24.

(Fig. 23) Red	Blue	(Fig. 24) Red	Blue
K4f1	K6f1	R1f6	K6f1
R1f2	N5b4	R1b4	N5b6
R1h4	P6h5	R1h9	K6b1
M3f1	K6b1	R9f4	K6f1
R4h9	P5h6	M3f1	N6f5
R9b2	N4f5	R9b4	N5b6
(draw)		R9b2	N6f7
		M1f3	
		(will win)	

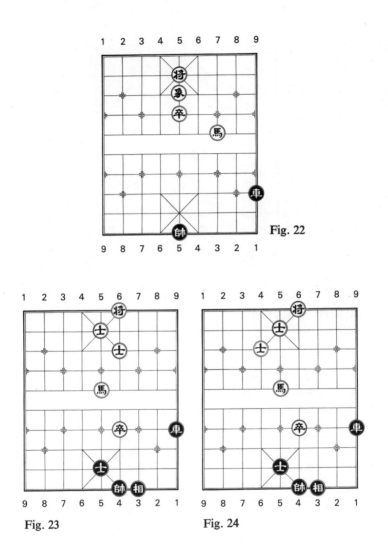

Fig. 22

Fig. 23

Fig. 24

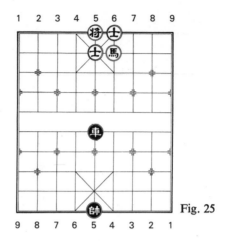

Fig. 25

7. R *vs.* N, S, S (Fig. 25)

One rook can always defeat one knight and two counsellors.

Red	Blue		Red	Blue
K5h6	N6b8		R8h3	K5h6
R5h8	S5b4		R3f2	K6f1
R8f4	N8f7		R3b4	N5f3
R8f1	S6f5		R3h4	S5f6
R8b3	S5b6		K5h4	S4f5
R8h3	N7b8		R4h7	N3f5
R3f2	N8f9		R7h3	N5f4
R3h6	S4f5		K4f1	S5f4
R6h8	S5b4		R3f3	K6b1
R8f1	S6f5		R3h6	N4b5
K6h5	N9f7		K4b1	
R8b2	N7f5		(will win)	

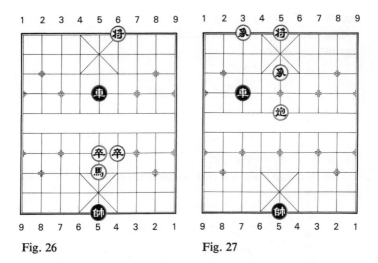

Fig. 26

Fig. 27

8. R *vs.* N, P, P (Fig. 26)

As long as the central lines are guarded properly, as they are here, one knight and two pawns can always force a draw against one rook.

Red	Blue
R5b2	K6f1
	(draw)

9. R *vs.* C, M, M (Fig. 27)

One cannon and two ministers can always force a draw against one rook.

Red	Blue
K5f1	K5f1
	(draw)

10. R *vs.* C, S, S (Fig. 28)

One cannon and two counsellors can always force a draw against one rook.

Red	Blue
R5f3	K5h6
(draw)	

11. R *vs.* C, S, P (Fig. 29)

One rook can always defeat one cannon, one counsellor, and one pawn.

Red	Blue	Red	Blue
R5h3	S5b4	K4h5	P6h7
R3f3	K6f1	R6b1	K6f1
R3h6	P6h5	R6h3	P7h6
R6f1	K6b1	R3b1	K6b1
K6h5	P5h6	R3f2	P6f1
K5h4	P6f1	K5f1	
K4f1	P6f1	(will win)	
K4b1	P6f1		

12. R *vs.* C, P, P (Fig. 30)

As long as the central lines are guarded properly, as they are here, one cannon and two pawns can always force a draw against one rook.

Red	Blue
R7h5	K5f1
K6f1	P5h4
(draw)	

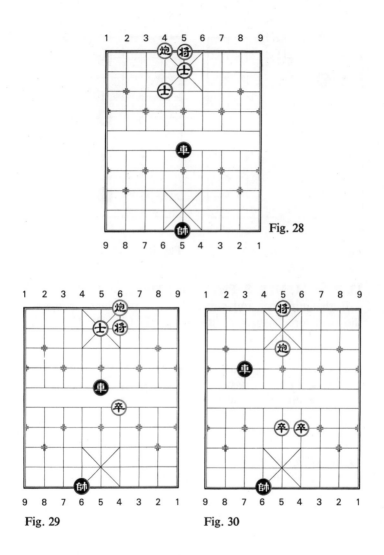

Fig. 28

Fig. 29

Fig. 30

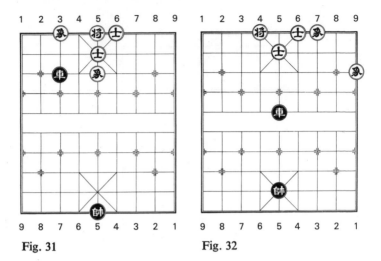

Fig. 31   Fig. 32

13. R *vs.* M, M, S, S (Figs. 31 and 32)

If the ministers and counsellors are positioned properly, they can force a draw against the rook (Fig. 31). If not, the rook can win (Fig. 32).

(Fig. 31) *Red*	*Blue*	(Fig. 32) *Red*	*Blue*
K5f1	K5h4	K5b1	K4h5
K5b1	K4h5	K5h6	
K5h6	S5b4	(will win)	
	(draw)		

14. R *vs.* M, M, P, P (Fig. 33)

In order for blue to force a draw, its two pawns have to be guarding the central lines.

Red	*Blue*
R5b2	K5f1
	(draw)

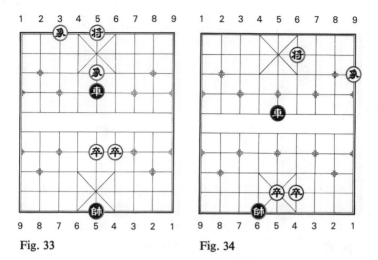

Fig. 33   Fig. 34

15. R *vs.* M, P, P (Fig. 34)

Usually one minister and two pawns cannot force a draw against one rook. This example is a special case resulting from the advantageous positioning of the pawns.

Red	Blue	Red	Blue
R5h1	M9b7	R4h5	K5h6
R1h3	M7f9	R5f1	K6f1
R3f3	K6b1	R5f2	M9b7
R3b1	K6f1	R5b2	M7f9
R3b1	K6b1	R5b2	M9b7
R3h4	K6h5	(draw)	

16. R *vs.* S, S, P, P (Fig. 35)

In order for blue to force a draw, its two pawns have to be guarding the central lines.

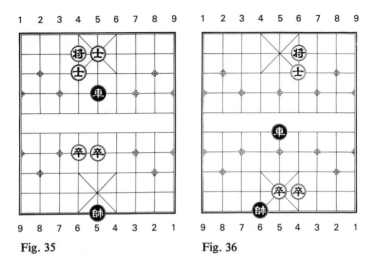

Fig. 35   Fig. 36

Red	Blue
R5b2	K4b1
(draw)	

17. R *vs.* S, P, P (Fig. 36)

Usually one counsellor and two pawns cannot force a draw against one rook. This example is a special case resulting from the advantageous positioning of the pawns.

Red	Blue		Red	Blue
R5f3	S6b5		R5f4	K6f1
R5b4	S5f6		R5f2	S6b5
R5h4	P6h7		R5h1	P6f1
R4h3	P7h6		R1b9	P6h5
R3h5	K6b1		R1h5	P5f1
			K6h5	
			(draw)	

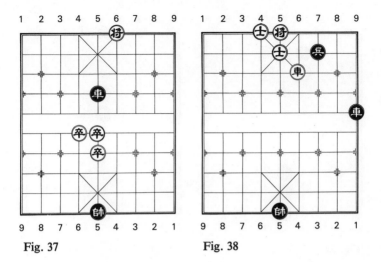

Fig. 37   Fig. 38

18. R *vs.* P, P, P (Fig. 37)

Blue will force a draw if the pieces are arranged in this way by the end-game.

Red	Blue
R5f2	P5h4
(draw)	

One Rook and One Pawn

1. R, P *vs.* R, S, S (Fig. 38)

Red will win if the pieces are arranged in this way by the end-game.

Red	Blue
R1f4	R6b2
R1h3	R6h7
P3f1	
(win)	

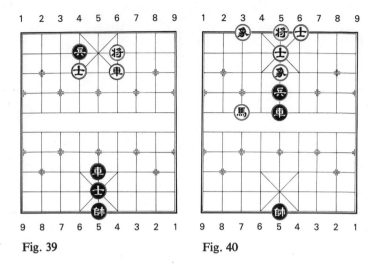

Fig. 39   Fig. 40

2. R, P, S *vs.* R, S (Fig. 39)

Blue will force a draw if the pieces are arranged in this way by the end-game.

Red	Blue
R5h2	K6b1
(draw)	

3. R, P *vs.* N, M, M, S, S (Fig. 40)

One rook and one pawn can always defeat one knight, two ministers, and two counsellors.

Red	Blue
P5f1	M3f5
R5f2	
(will win)	

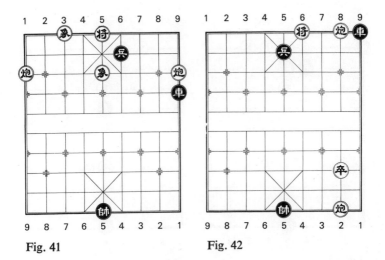

Fig. 41   Fig. 42

4. R, P *vs.* C, C, M, M (Fig. 41)

Blue will force a draw if the pieces are arranged in this way by the end-game. The cannons prevent the rook from advancing.

Red	Blue
R1h2	C9h8
R2h6	C1h4
(draw)	

5. R, P *vs.* C, C, P (Fig. 42)

Blue will force a draw if the pieces are arranged in this way by the end-game. The cannons guard the king from the rook's attack.

Red	Blue
R1b2	C8f2
R1b6	fCb1
(draw)	

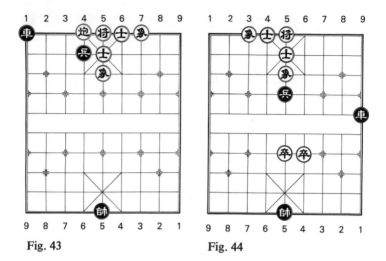

Fig. 43　　　　　　　　　Fig. 44

6. R, P *vs.* C, M, M, S, S (Fig. 43)

One cannon, two ministers, and two counsellors can always force a draw against one rook and one pawn.

Red	Blue
K5f1	M7f9
(draw)	

7. R, P *vs.* M, M, S, S, P, P (Fig. 44)

In order for blue to force a draw, its two pawns have to be guarding the central lines.

Red	Blue
R1h5	K5h6
(draw)	

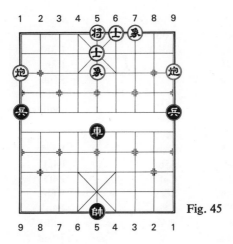

Fig. 45

One Rook and Two Pawns (Fig. 45)

R, P, P *vs.* C, C, M, M, S, S

Red will win if the pieces are arranged in this way by the end-game.

Red	Blue		Red	Blue
P1f1	C9h7		P4f1	S6f5
P9f1	C1h3		P4f1	C8b2
P9h8	C3h1		P6h7	M9f7
P1h2	C7h9		P7f1	M7f9
P2h3	C9h8		R8b3	C8h7
P8h7	C8h9		R8h2	C7h6
P7h6	C1h2		P7f1	C6h7
P3h4	C9h8		P7h6*d	S5f6
P4h5*a	M5f7		R2h4	S4f5
R5h8*b	C2h5		P4h5	S6b5
P5h4*c	M7b9		R4f2	S5f6
R8f5	S5b4		R4b1	C7h6

K 帥 (将) · R 車 · N 馬 · C 炮 · S 士 · M 相 (象) · P 兵 (卒) · **73**

Red	Blue		Red	Blue
R4f1	C6h7		K5h6	C4f1
P6h5	K5h4		R3b3	C4b1
R4f1			R3h4	C9b1
(win)			P5h6	S5f4
			R4f3	
a.	M5b3		(will win)	
R5h8	M7f5			
P5f1	M3f5		**c.**	K5h4
P6h5	C2h4		R8f5	K4f1
P5f1	S5b4		P4f1	M7f9
R8h5	C4f1		P4f1	C8h7
P5h6	S6f5		R8b1	K4b1
P6f1	C8h6		P4h5	S6f5
P6f1	K5h4		R8h5	C7h8
R5f4	C6f3		R5h4	K4h5
R5b4	C6b1		R4b1	C8f2
R5h6	C4b2		P6f1	C5f2
R6h4	C6h5		P6f1	M9b7
R4f5	C5b4		R4f1	M7b5
R4h5			R4b3	
(win)			(will win)	
b.	C2h7		**d.**	C7f2
R8h2	C8h9		P4h5	S4f5
R2f3	C7f1		R2f2	S5b4
R2h3	C7h4		R2h4	C7b2
R3f2	C4b1		K5h4	S4f5
R3b4	K5h4		R4h5	
P5f1	C9f3		(win)	
R3f4	K4f1			

One Rook and One Knight

R, N *vs.* R, S, S (Fig. 46)

Blue will force a draw if the pieces are arranged in this way by the end-game.

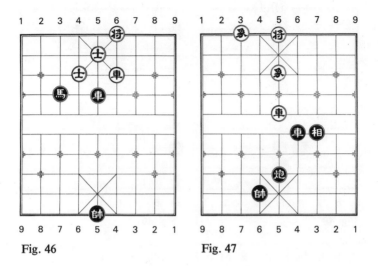

Fig. 46   Fig. 47

Red	Blue
N7b5	R6f2
(draw)	

One Rook and One Cannon

1. R, C, M *vs.* R, M, M (Fig. 47)

Blue will force a draw if the pieces are arranged in this way by the end-game.

Red	Blue
R4f4	R5f2
R4h7	K5h6
(draw)	

K帥(将)・R車・N馬・C炮・S士・M相(象)・P兵(卒)・**75**

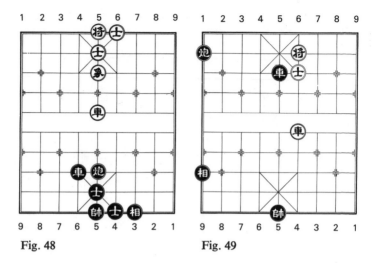

Fig. 48   Fig. 49

2. R, C, M, S, S *vs.* R, M, S, S (Fig. 48)

Red will win if the pieces are arranged in this way by the end-game.

Red	Blue	Red	Blue
K5h6	R5f1	S4b5	R5h3
S5f4	R5b2	C5f7	S5f6
C5b2	R5f2	C5b5	
R6f3	R5b2	(will win)	

3. R, C, M *vs.* R, S (Fig. 49)

Red will win if the pieces are arranged in this way by the end-game.

Red	Blue	Red	Blue
C9b1	R6f3	K5f1	R6f4
M9f7	R6b3	M7b5	S6b5

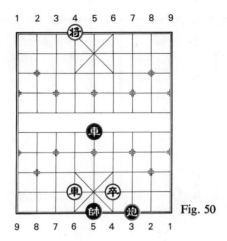

Fig. 50

Red	Blue		Red	Blue
M5f3	S5f6		R5b1	K6b1
M3b1	R6b2		C4h3	R8b5
C9b7	R6f2		R5b2	R8h6
C9h5	K6b1		C3f9	R6f5
R5b1	K6f1		K5f1	R6b5
R5f3	R6h8		R5f3	K6f1
C5h3	R8h9		C3h4	R6h4
K5b1	R9h8		R5b3	
C3h4	S6b5		(will win)	

4. R, C *vs.* R, P (Fig. 50)

Blue will force a draw if the pieces are arranged in this way by the end-game.

Red	Blue
R5f1	K4f1
(draw)	

K 帥 (将) · R 車 · N 馬 · C 炮 · S 士 · M 相 (象) · P 兵 (卒) · **77**

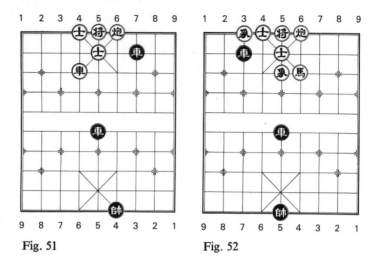

Fig. 51   Fig. 52

Two Rooks

1. R, R *vs.* R, C, S, S (Fig. 51)

Blue will force a draw if the pieces are arranged in this way by the end-game.

Red	Blue
R3f1	R4h6
K4h5	R6f2
(draw)	

2. R, R *vs.* N, C, M, M, S, S (Fig. 52)

Blue will force a draw if the pieces are arranged in this way by the end-game.

Red	Blue
R7h6	C6f1
R6b2	C6b1
(draw)	

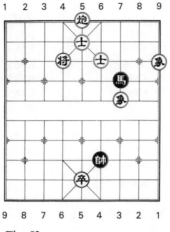

Fig. 53

One Knight

1. N *vs.* C, M, M, S, S, bottom P* (Fig. 53)

The knight can force a draw here. In order to do so, it must prevent the blue king from occupying line 5. If the king is able to move to line 5, the knight will lose.

Red	Blue	Red	Blue
N3f2	K4h5	K4h5	C8b1
N2b3	K5h4	N3b1	C8f2
N3f2	P5h4	N1b2	K5h4
N2b3	C5h8	N2f4	C8b4
K4h5	C8f3	N4f3	C8f4
K5h4	K4b1	K5h4	C8b1
K4h5	K4b1	K4h5	K4h5
K5h4	K4h5	N3f2	K5h4

* A bottom pawn is one which has passed the opponent's king.

Red	Blue		Red	Blue
N2b3	S5f4		N3b1	M7b5
N3f2	S6b5		K5h4	K4h5
N2b3	S5b6		K4h5	K5h4
N3f2	C8b1		K5h4	M5f3
N2f4	S4b5		K4h5	S6b5
N4b3	S5f6		K5h4	K4f1
N3b2	K4f1		N1f3	M9f7
N2b3	K4f1		N3f2	C5h7
N3b1	C8b2		N2b3	
N1f2	C8h5			(draw)
N2f3	K4b1			

2. N *vs.* C, M, M, S, S (Fig. 54)

This is the only arrangement in which one knight can force a draw against one cannon, two ministers, and two counsellors.

Red	Blue
K4f1	C7b1
N3f2	
	(draw)

3. N *vs.* M (Figs. 55 and 56)

One minister can force a draw against one knight only if the minister and its king are on opposite sides of vertical line 5 (Fig. 55). If they are on the same side of line 5, the knight will win (Fig. 56).

(Fig. 55) Red	Blue	(Fig. 56) Red	Blue
N6f4	K6f1	N7b6	M9b7
N4f6	M3f5	K5f1	K6f1
N6f5	M5b3	N6b4	K6b1
	(draw)	N4f3	
		(will win)	

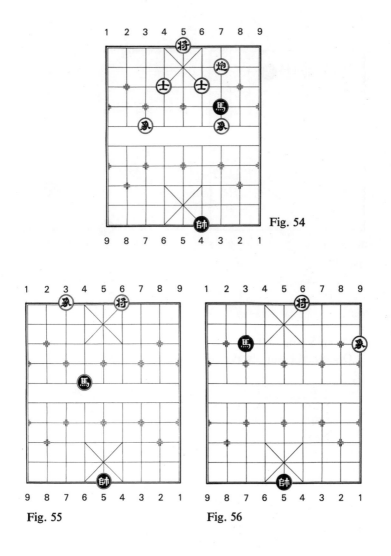

Fig. 54

Fig. 55

Fig. 56

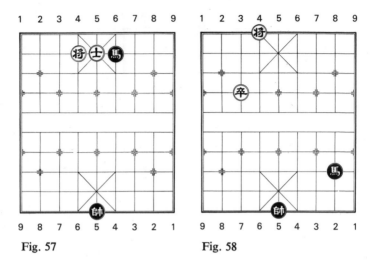

Fig. 57   Fig. 58

4. N *vs.* S (Fig. 57)

One knight can always defeat one counsellor.

Red	Blue		Red	Blue
N4b5	K4f1		N4f6	S5b6
N5f3	S5f6		N6f8	S6f5
N3b4	S6b5		N8f7	
			(will win)	

5. N *vs.* P (Fig. 58)

Since the pawn has not crossed the river, the knight can win (depending on the arrangement), as shown here. If the pawn had already crossed the river, it would have been able to force a draw.

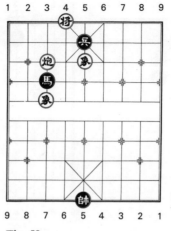

Fig. 59

Red	Blue		Red	Blue
N2f3	P3f1		N7b9	K5b1
N3f5	K4h5		K4f1	K5f1
K5h4	K5f1		N9f8	P3f1
K4f1	K5f1		N8b6	
N5f7	K5b1		(will win)	

One Knight and One Pawn

1. N, P _vs._ C, M, M (Fig. 59)

Blue will force a draw if the pieces are arranged in this way by the end-game.

Red	Blue
K5f1	M5b7
(draw)	

K 帥 (将)・R 車・N 馬・C 炮・S 士・M 相 (象)・P 兵 (卒)・**83**

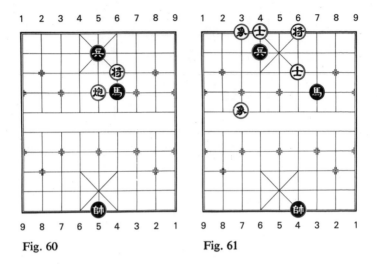

Fig. 60   Fig. 61

2. N, bottom P *vs.* C (Fig. 60)

In general, one knight and one pawn are able to defeat one cannon. However, as shown here, if the pawn has advanced beyond the opponent's king, the cannon can force a draw.

Red	Blue
K5f1	K6h5
(draw)	

3. N, P *vs.* M, M, S, S (Fig. 61)

One knight and one pawn are usually drawn by two ministers and two counsellors.

Red	Blue
N3b5	K6f1
(draw)	

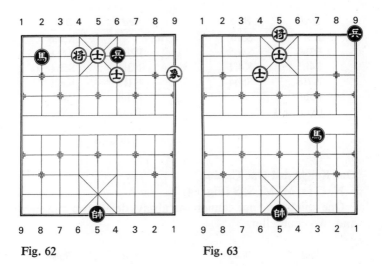

Fig. 62   Fig. 63

4. N, P *vs.* M, S, S (Fig. 62)

Blue will force a draw if the pieces are arranged in this way by the end-game.

Red	Blue
K5f1	M9f7
(draw)	

5. N, bottom P *vs.* S, S (Fig. 63)

Red will win if the pieces are arranged in this way by the end-game.

Red	Blue		Red	Blue
P1h2*[a]	K5h4		K5f1	K4f1
P2h3	K4h5		N4b6	K4b1
N3f4	K5h4		N6f7	K4f1

Red	Blue		Red	Blue
K5f1	S5f6	a.		K5h6
P3h4	S4b5		P2h3	K6f1
P4h5	K4f1		N3f1	S5b4
N7f8	S5b4		N1f3	K6f1
P5h6			P3h4	S4f5
(will win)			P4h5	S5b6
			P5h4	
			(will win)	

One Knight and One Cannon

N, C *vs.* M, M, S, S (Fig. 64)

One knight and one cannon can always defeat two ministers and two counsellors.

Red	Blue		Red	Blue
C4h5	K5h4		N6f7	K4h5
N7f6*a,b	S5f6		C6h5	S5f6
N6f7*c	M5f7		N7f8	K5h6
N7f8	K4h5		N8b6	
N8b6	K5f1		(will win)	
N6b5	K5h6			
K5h4	M7f9	b.		M5f7
C5h4	K6h5		N6f7	S5f6
N5f4	M7b5		N7f8	K4h5
N4f2	K5b1		N8b6	K5f1
C4h5	S6f5		N6b5	K5h6
N2b4	K5h4		C5h4	K6h5
C5f6			K5h4	M7b5
(will win)			N5f4	
			(will win)	

	Red	Blue
a.		S5f4
	C5h6	S6f5
	K5h4	M5b3

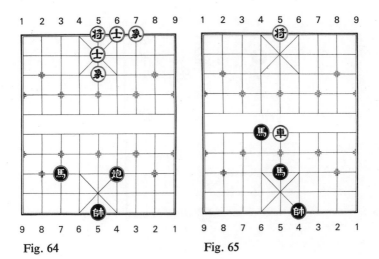

Fig. 64

Fig. 65

	Red	Blue
c.		M5f3
	N7f8	K4f1
	C5h9	M3b1
	N8b7	K4b1
	N7f9	
	(will win)	

Two Knights

1. N, N *vs.* R (Fig. 65)

If the two knights are chained together at this stage of the game, they can force a draw against the rook.

Red	Blue
K4f1	K5f1
(draw)	

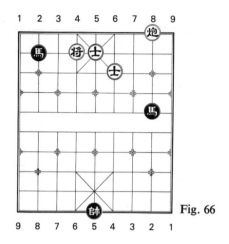

Fig. 66

2. N, N *vs.* C, S, S (Fig. 66)

Two knights can always defeat one cannon and two counsellors.

Red	Blue		Red	Blue
N2f4	C8f1		fNb9	K4b1
N4b6	S5b6		N9f8	C8h3
N8b7	K4b1		N7f9	
N6f7	K4f1		(will win)	

3. N, N *vs.* N, S, S (Fig. 67)

Two knights can always defeat one knight and two counsellors.

Red	Blue		Red	Blue
N6f7	N8f6		N2b4	N6b4
N7f8	K4f1		K5h6	S5b6

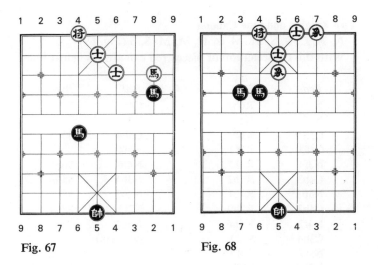

Fig. 67　　　　　　　Fig. 68

Red	Blue
N4f2	S6b5
K6f1	
(will win)	

4. N, N *vs.* M, M, S, S (Fig. 68)

Two knights can always defeat two ministers and two coun-sellors.

Red	Blue
N7f8	K4h5
N6f7	K5h4
N7b5	K4h5
N5f3	
(win)	

Two Knights and One Cannon

N, N, C, S, S, M, M *vs.* R, M, M, S, S (Fig. 69)

With this combination of pieces, red can always defeat blue.

Red	Blue		Red	Blue
N5b7*a	R6h3		C4h3	R7h9
N7f5	K5h6		N4f3	K5h6
C5h4	K6h5		C3h4	S4b5
C4f3	R3f2		N3f4	S5f6
N3f4	R3h7		N4f6	S6b5
C4b3	R7b2		N3b4	S5f6
N5b3*b	R7b1		N4b2	S6b5
C4h3	R7h9		N2f3	K6f1
N4f3	K5h6		N3b1	
C3h4	K6f1		(will win)	
N3f2	R9f3			
N2b4	S5f6	**b.**		R7b2
N4f5	K6h5		N3f2	S5f6
N5b4	R9h4		N2f4	K5f1
N3b2	R4b2		rNb5	R6f1
N2f4*c	M3f5		N4b5	R7h5
C4h5	K5h6		fNb3	K5b1
N4f5	R4h3		N3f4	S6f5
N4f2	R3h7		C4h5	R5h3
N2b3	K6f1		N4f3	K5h4
C5h4	R7b1		C5h6	R3h7
N5b4	R7h6		N5f4	K4f1
C4f4			N4b6	S5f4
(will win)			N3b4	R7f3
			N6b5	S4b5
a.	R6h7		N4f6	K4f1
N7f6	K5h6		N5f6	R7h4
C5h4	S5f4		N6f4	
N6b5	R7b1		(win)	
N5f4	K6h5			

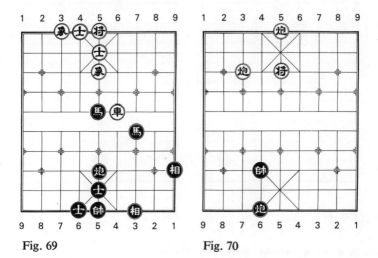

Fig. 69   Fig. 70

	Red	Blue		Red	Blue
c.		M3f1		N6f8	S4f5
	rNf6	K5f1		N4b5	
	C4h5	K5h4		(win)	
	C5h3	M1b3			
	C3f5	M3f5			

One Cannon

1. C *vs.* C, C (Fig. 70)

One cannon can always force a draw against two cannons.

Red	Blue
K6b1	
(draw)	

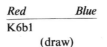

K 帥 (将)・R 車・N 馬・C 炮・S 士・M 相 (象)・P 兵 (卒) ・ **91**

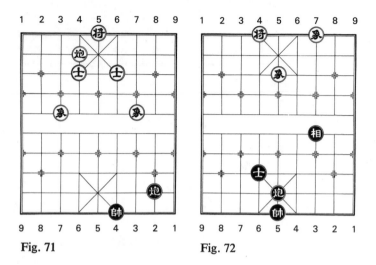

Fig. 71   Fig. 72

2. C vs. C, M, M, S, S (Fig. 71)

One cannon can always force a draw against one cannon, two ministers, and two counsellors.

Red	Blue
C2h1	C4h6
C1h4	C6h7
C4h2	
(draw)	

3. C, M, S vs. M, M (Fig. 72)

Two ministers can always force a draw against one cannon, one minister, and one counsellor.

Red	Blue
C5h6	K4h5
C6h3	K5h4
(draw)	

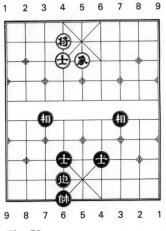

Fig. 73

4. C, M, M, S, S *vs.* M, S (Fig. 73)

One minister and one counsellor can always force a draw against one cannon, two ministers, and two counsellors.

Red	Blue
C6h5	S4b5
C5h4	M5f3
C4h6	S5f4
C6h7	M3b1
S6b5	K4h5
S5b4	K5b1
C7h4	M1f3
K6f1	M3b1
S4f5	M1f3
C4b1	M3b1
M3b5	M1f3
S5f6	M3b1

Red	Blue
C4h6	S4b5
C6h5	M1f3
K6h5	S5b6
C5h4	M3b1
C4h7	K5f1
(draw)	

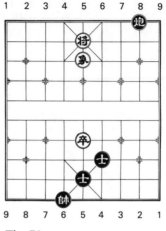

Fig. 74

5. C, S, S *vs.* M, P (Fig. 74)

One cannon and two counsellors can always defeat one pawn and one minister. (However, one cannon and one counsellor may not succeed because the single counsellor is vulnerable to the pawn.)

Red	Blue		Red	Blue
C2b9	P5h4		K5b1	K4f1
C2h5	P4h3		C5h2	
K6f1	P3h4		(will win)	
C5h6*ᵃ	P4h5			
K6f1	K5b1	**a.**		P4h3
C6h5	P5h4		K6f1	M5f7
K6h5	K5h4		C6h5	M7b5
S5f6	P4f1		K6h5	P3h4
			S5b6	
			(will win)	

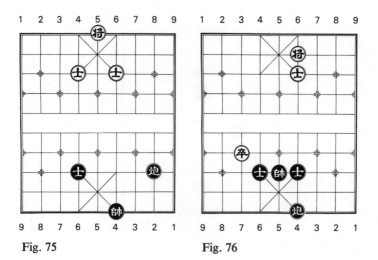

Fig. 75　　　　　　　　Fig. 76

6. C, S vs. S, S (Fig. 75)

One cannon and one counsellor can always defeat two counsellors.

Red	Blue	Red	Blue
C2b1	S4b5	C4h5	S5f4
K4h5	K5h6	C5h6	S6b5
C2h6	K6h5	C6b1	
C6h4	K5h4	(will win)	

7. C, S, S vs. S, P (Fig. 76)

One counsellor and one pawn can always force a draw against one cannon and two counsellors.

Red	Blue
K5b1	P3h4
K5h4	S6b5
(draw)	

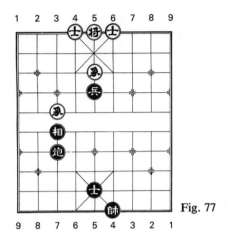

Fig. 77

One Cannon and One Pawn

1. C, P, M, S *vs.* M, M, S, S (Fig. 77)

This combination generally results in a win for red (shown here), provided that the red pawn is on the first or second line on the opposite side of the river.

Red	Blue
P5h6	M3b1
P6f1*[a],[b]	M5f7
C7h5	K5f1
S5f6	M1f3
C5b3	K5b1
P6f1	M3b1
C5f6	M7b9
K4h5	M9f7
K5h6	M7b9
S6b5	M9b7
S5f4	M7f9

Red	Blue
C5h8	S4f5
K6h5	M9b7
C8h2	M1f3
K5f1	M3b1
C2f3	
(will win)	

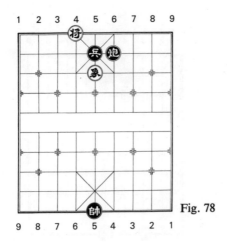

Fig. 78

	Red	Blue		Red	Blue
a.		S4f5	**b.**		S6f5
	P6h5	K5h4		C7h5	M1b3
	C7b3	K4h5		P6h5	M3f1
	S5f6	K5h4		S5f6	M1b3
	K4h5	K4h5		C5b3	M3f1
	K5f1	K5h4		P5f1	K5f1
	P5f1	S6f5		M7b5	K5h4
	C7h6	K4h5		C5h6	K4h5
	C6h5			C6f9	
	(will win)			(will win)	

2. C, P *vs.* M (Fig. 78)

One minister can always force a draw against one cannon and one pawn.

Red	Blue
K5f1	M5f3
(draw)	

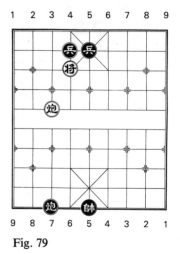

Fig. 79

One Cannon and Two Pawns

1. C, P, P vs. C (Fig. 79)

One cannon and two pawns can always defeat one cannon.

Red	Blue		Red	Blue
C7f4	C3b1		C6h5	K5h4
C7f1	C3b3		K4h5	
C7f1	C3h5		(will win)	
K5h4	C5h3			
C7h4*[a]	C3h6	**a.**		C3h5
K4h5	C6f2		C4f3	C5h3
C4h7	C6b2		C4h6	K4h5
C7f3	C6h5		C6h5	K5h4
K5h4	C5h6		K4h5	
C7h6	K4h5		(will win)	

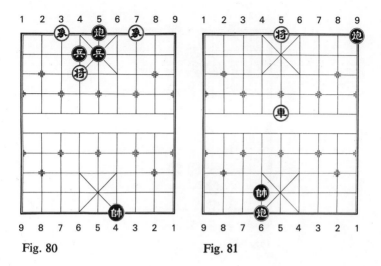

Fig. 80   Fig. 81

2. C, P, P *vs.* **M, M (Fig. 80)**

One cannon and two pawns can always defeat two ministers.

Red	Blue
K4h5	
(will win)	

Two Cannons

1. C, C *vs.* **R (Fig. 81)**

Two cannons can always force a draw against one rook.

Red	Blue
C1h2	R5f3
(draw)	

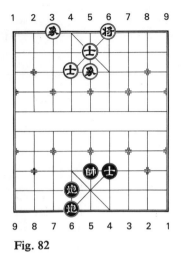

Fig. 82

2. C, C, S vs. M, M, S, S (Fig. 82)

Two cannons and one counsellor can always defeat two ministers and two counsellors.

Red	Blue		Red	Blue
fCh4	K6h5		rCh5	K5h4
S4b5	S5f6		C4h6	M5f7
C6h4	S6b5		C5f3	
K5h4	M5b7		(will win)	
S5f6	M3f5			

3. C, C, M, M vs. M, M (Fig. 83)

Two cannons and two ministers can always defeat two ministers. (Two cannons with one minister or with no ministers will be drawn by two ministers, however.)

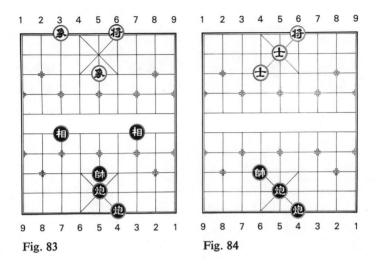

Fig. 83   Fig. 84

Red	Blue		Red	Blue
C5h4	K6h5		C7h5	K5h4
K5h4	K5f1		K4h5	M9b7
fCh5	M5f7		fCh6	
C4h3	M7b9		(will win)	
C3h7	M3f1			

4. C, C *vs*. S, S (Fig. 84)

Two cannons can always defeat two counsellors.

Red	Blue
C5h4	K6h5
K6h5	K5h4
K5h4	K4h5
fCh5	
(will win)	

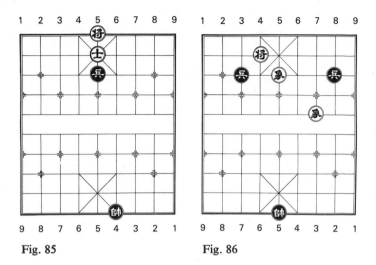

Fig. 85   Fig. 86

One Pawn

P *vs.* S (Fig. 85)

One counsellor (or one minister) can always force a draw against one pawn. (One pawn unopposed, however, can win.)

Red	Blue		Red	Blue
K4h5	S5b6		K6h5	S4f5
K5h6	S6f5		P4h5	S5b4
K6f1	S5b4		(draw)	
P5h4	K5h6			

Two Pawns

1. P, P *vs.* M, M (Fig. 86)

If the two pawns are on the first or second line on the opposite side of the river, they can always defeat two ministers.

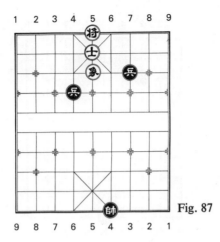

Fig. 87

However, if they have gone beyond the second line, as shown here, the ministers will always be able to force a draw.

Red	Blue
K5f1	M5b7
P7f1	K4f1
(draw)	

2. P, P vs. M, S (Fig. 87)

One minister and one counsellor can always force a draw against two pawns.

Red	Blue		Red	Blue
P3f1	K5h4		K6f1	M5f7
P3h4	K4f1		K6h5	S5b4
K4h5	S5b4		K5h6	S4f5
K5h6	S4f5		(draw)	

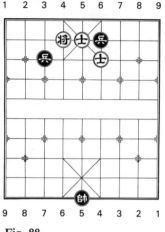

Fig. 88

3. P, P *vs.* S, S (Fig. 88)

If the two pawns are on the first or second line on the opposite side of the river, they can always defeat two counsellors. However, if they have gone beyond the second line, as shown here, the two counsellors will always be able to force a draw.

Red	*Blue*
K5f1	S5b4
(draw)	

Three Pawns

P, P, P *vs.* M, M, S, S (Fig. 89)

If the three pawns are on the first or second line on the opposite side of the river, they can always defeat two ministers and two counsellors.

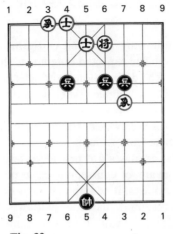

Fig. 89

Red	Blue
P6h7	M3f5
P7f1	M5f3
P7f1	M7b9
P7h6	M9f7
P3f1	M3b5
K5h4	M7b9
P4f1	K6b1
P4f1	K6h5

Red	Blue
P4h5	S4f5
P3f1	M5f3
K4h5	M3b5
P3h4	S5f6
K5h6	S6b5
P6h5	
(win)	

8 · MID-GAME AND END-GAME EXERCISES

In each of the following mid- and end-game exercises, it is red's turn to move. The expected outcome is shown at the top of each diagram. The designation "win" means that red is expected to win. "Draw" implies that red cannot win even if it makes the best moves (provided, of course, that blue doesn't do anything foolish); however, red in these cases should be able to prevent blue from winning.

Answers to the exercises are provided, beginning on page 127. Because there are, of course, numerous possible solutions to each of the exercises, it is impossible to enumerate all of them. In some cases, more than one solution is shown. In most of the answers for the "win" (red win) games, the list(s) of moves show all the way to the winning move, and those for "draw" games all the way to a draw situation. Thus, the designation "win" or "draw" is not shown at the end of the answer for such cases. In several cases, variations giving a re ʳlt other than the designated outcome have been included for ɪne sake of interest; the outcome is explicitly stated at the end of each of the variations, including those leading to the designated outcome, in such cases. Finally, examples in which the final moves to the win are not shown are noted with "will win" in the appropriate column.

1. Win

 2. Win

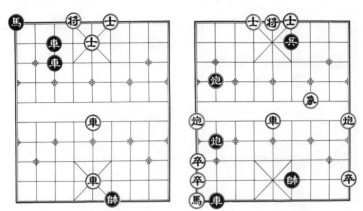

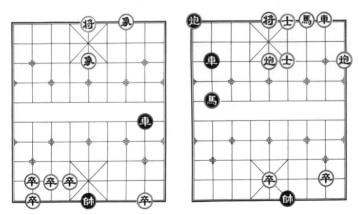

3. Win

4. Win

5. Win

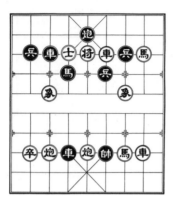

6. Win

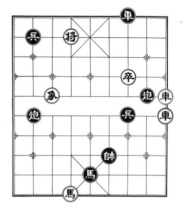

7. Draw

8. Win

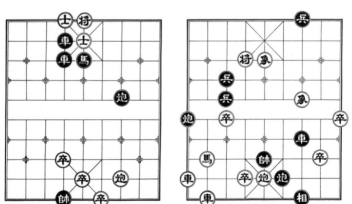

9. Win

10. Win

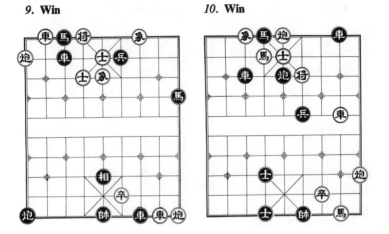

11. Draw

12. Win

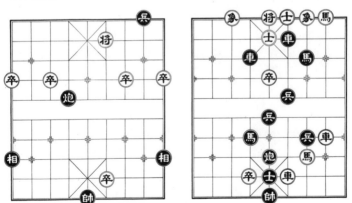

13. Draw

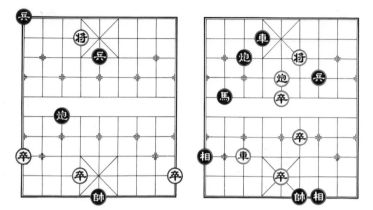

14. Draw

15. Draw

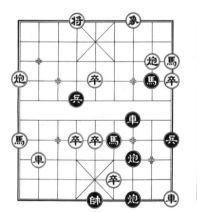

16. Win

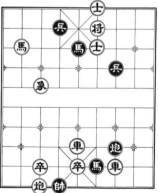

17. Win

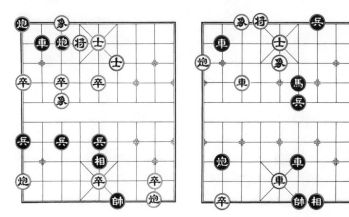

18. Draw

19. Win

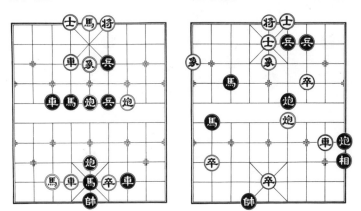

20. Draw

21. Win

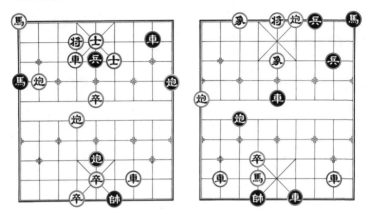

22. Win

23. Win

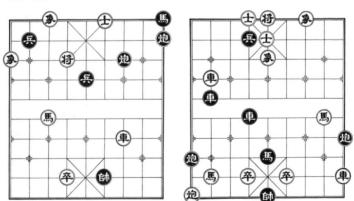

24. Win

25. Draw

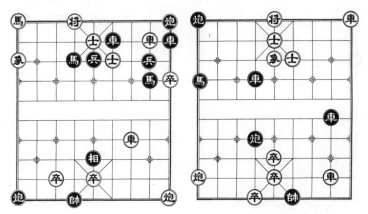

26. Win

27. Win

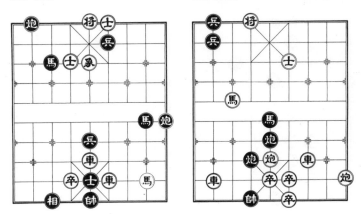

28. Win

29. Win

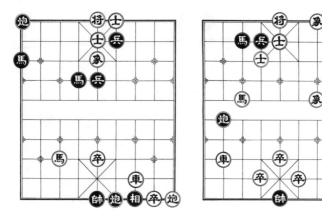

30. Win

31. Win

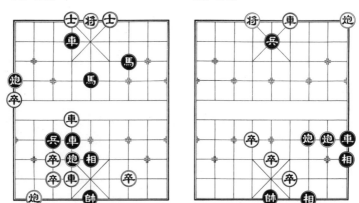

32. Win

33. Draw

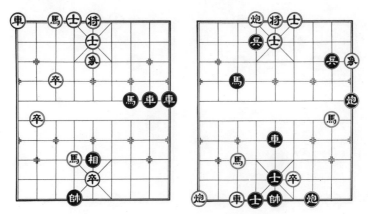

34. Win

35. Win

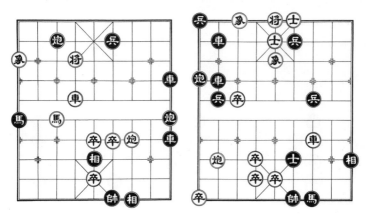

36. Win

37. Win

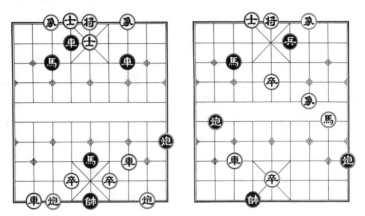

38. Draw

39. Win

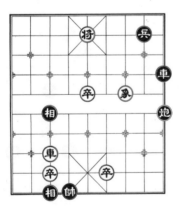

40. Blue wins

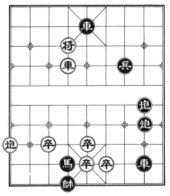

41. Draw

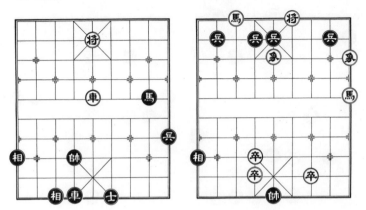

42. Draw

43. Draw

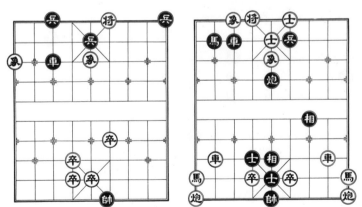

44. Win

45. Win

46. Draw

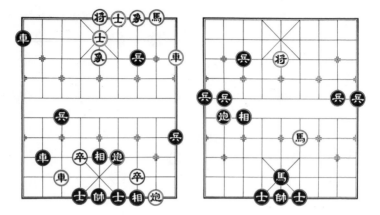

47. Draw

48. Draw

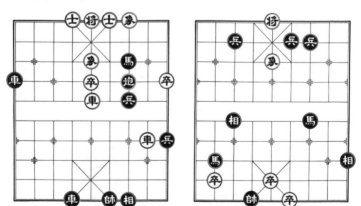

49. Draw

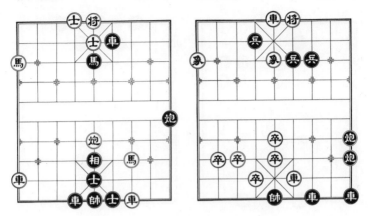

50. Win

51. Draw

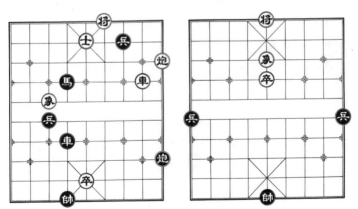

52. Draw

53. Win

54. Win

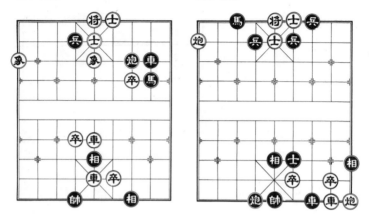

55. Win

56. Draw

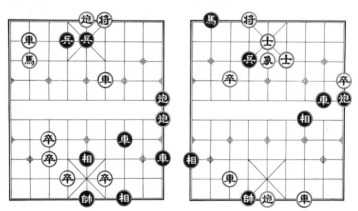

57. Draw

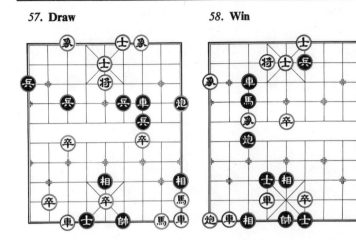

58. Win

59. Win

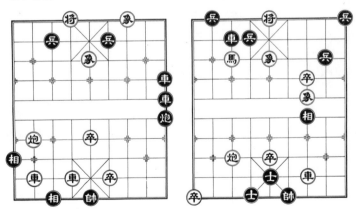

60. Draw

61. Win

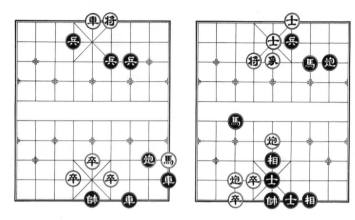

62. Draw

63. Draw

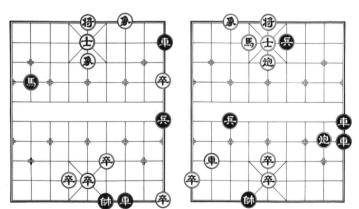

64. Draw

65. Draw

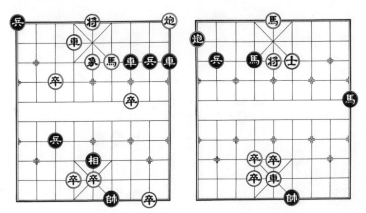

66. Draw

67. Draw

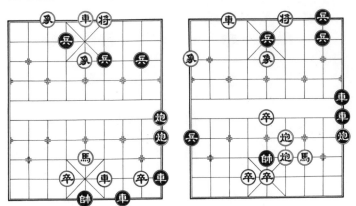

68. Draw

69. Win

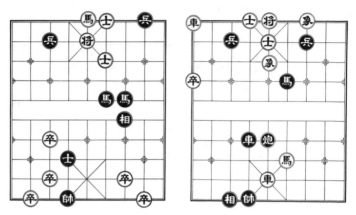

70. Win

71. Win

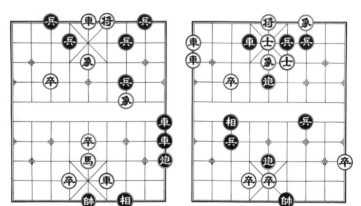

72. Draw

73. Win

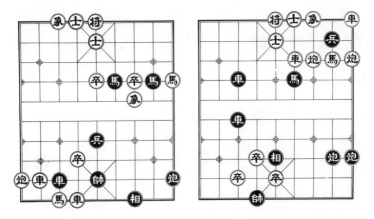

74. Win

75. Draw

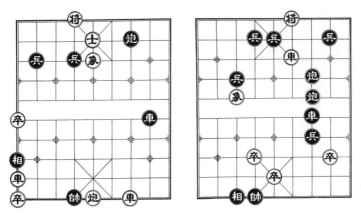

76. Draw

77. Win

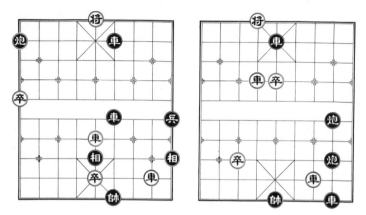

78. Draw

79. Win

80. Draw

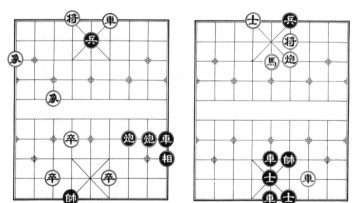

ANSWERS TO THE EXERCISES

	Red	Blue		Red	Blue
1.	R7f1	K4f1		R6f1	K5f1
	R7f1	K4f1		K6h5	M7f9
	rRh6	K4b1		R6h1	M9f7
	N9b8	K4f1		R1b3	P3h4
	R7b2	K4b1		R1h5	P4h3
	R7b1	K4f1		R5b1	K5h4
	N8f7	K4b1		R5h6	K4h5
	R7h6	S5f4		R6h3	
	R6f1				
			4.	R8f2	K5f1
2.	R8h5	R5f4		R8b1	K5b1
	fCh2	R5h8		N8f7	C5h4
	C2h5	C9h2		N7f8	C4b2
	C8h5	C2h5		N8b6	K5f1
	fCh3	C5h7		N6b8	K5f1
	C3h7	R8h3		C9b2	C4f2
	C7h5	C1h5		N8b6	C4b1
	fCh2	M7b5		R8b1	C4f1
	C2h3	C7h6		R8h6	K5b1
	C5f4	C5b2		R6h4	K5h4
	C3f3			R4h6	K4h5
				R6h1	K5h4
3.	R2b4	P2h3		R1h6	K4h5
	R2f1	P3h4		R6h4	K5h4
	K5h4	P4h3		N6f8	K4h5
	K4f1	P3h4		N8f7	K5h4
	K4f1	P4h3		R4h6	
	K4h5	P3h4			
	R2f3	P4h3	5.	R7h6*a	K5h4
	R2h9	K5h4		P8h7*b	K4b1
	R9h6	K4h5		P7f1*c	K4f1
	K5h6	K5f1		N6b5	K4h5
	R6f4	K5b1		P4f1	K5b1

Red	Blue
P4f1	K5b1
P4f1	K5f1
P7h6	K5f1
P3h4	

a.

Red	Blue
	K5b1
R6h5	K5f1
P4f1	K5h4
N6b5	

b.

Red	Blue
	C3b5
N6f4	K4h5
P4h5	K5b1
R6f6	

c.

Red	Blue
	C3b6
N6f4	K4h5
R6f6	K5f1
P4h5	

6.

Red	Blue
P8h7	K4f1
R3b2	M3b5
C8h1	R9h8
N5f4	R8h3
C1b2	R3h9
C1h2	R9h6
R3h4	R6b2
C2f5	N4b3
K4h5	N3b4
K5h6	R6h8
N4f5	

7.

Red	Blue
R6f1	S5b4
R6f2	K5f1
R6h5	K5h6

Red	Blue
N5b3	C7b5
R5b8	C7h4
C3h6	P4h5
C6h7	P5f1
C7b5	P6h5
C7h5	P5f1
K6h5	

8.

Red	Blue
R3f2*[a]	M5f7
P7f1	K4b1
fPf1*[b]	K4b1
C9h1	M7b9
C1h2	M9b7
C2f5	M7f9
C4f8	M9b7
C4b1	M7f9
C2b1	R1b8
fPh6	

a.

Red	Blue
	K4b1
R3f3	K4b1
C9h1	M5b7
R3f1	K4f1
R3b1	R4b1
C9f5	N2b4
C4f8	

b.

Red	Blue
	K4f1
rPf1	N2b1
rPf1	

9.

Red	Blue
C9h6	K4h5
R7h5	S4b5
P4h5	K5h4
N7b6	C1h4

Red	Blue		Red	Blue
N6b8	C4h1		C4b2	P6f1
N8b6	C1h4		K5f1	
N6f5	C4h1			
N5b6	C1h4	**a.**		P9f1
N6b7	C4h3		C9f3	P7f1
N7b6	C3h4		P2h3	P9h8
N6b4	C4h3		C9h4	P6h7
R3f9			K5f1	P7f1
			K5f1	P3f1
10. C5f2	K6b1		K5b1	rPh8
R2h4	S5b6		K5f1	fPf1
S5b9	K6h5		M1b3	rPh7
R7h5	K5f1		K5b1	P8h7
S6f5	C9h5		M3f1	rPf1
S5f4	K5h4		K5f1	
N6b4	C5b6			
C5h6	K4h5	**12.** C5f4	S5f6
N4b3	K5h6		R6h5	K5h4
P4f1	K6h5		R4h6	K4f1
P4h5	K5h6		N3f4	K4b1
P5f1			R5h6	K4h5
			N4b5	S6b5
11. C6b4	P9f1		N5f3	K5h6
C6h9	P9f1		R6h4	S5f6
C9f5*[a]	P7f1		C5h4	S6b5
C9f3	P9f1		C4b5	S5f6
P2h3	P9f1		P4h5	S6b5
C9h4	P6h7		N6f4	S5f6
K5f1	rPf1		N4f2	S6b5
K5f1	P9h8		N2f4	S5f6
K5b1	P8h7		N4f6	S6b5
K5f1	P3f1		N3b4	S5f6
K5b1	rPh6		N4f2	S6b5
C6b5	rPh6		N2f4	S5f6
C6b1	P7h6		N4f2	S6b5

Red	Blue		Red	Blue
N2b3			M9b7	
13. C7b3*a	P4h3	**15.**	R3f5	K4f1
K5f1	P3h4		N2f4	K4h5
K5f1	P1h2		R3b1	K5f1
P9h8	P2h3		C3f5	K5h6
P8h7	P3h4		C3h1	C8f7
K5h4			C3f7	C8b7
(draw)			C3b7	C8f7
			C3f7	C8b7
a.	P1h2			
C7h1	P2h3	**16.**	N5f6	R5b7
C1f8	P3h4		C3h4	S6b5
C1h5	rPh3		P3h4	S5f6
K5h4	P3h4		P6h5	K6h5
K4f1	rPh3		N6b7	K5h6
K4f1	P3h4		P4h3	S6b5
C5h1			N7b5	M3b5
(will win)			P3h4	S5f6
			P4f1	K6h5
14. P3h4	K6h5		N5f7	C3b7
P4h5	K5h6		C4h5	M5b3
P5h4	K6h5		N4f5	C3h5
P4f1	K5h6		N5f4	C5h4
N8f6	K6h5		P4h5	K5h4
N6b4	K5h6		P5h6	K4b1
N4f2	K6h5		C5h6	N2b4
N2f3	K5h6		P6f1	K4f1
N3f5	K6h5		N4f6	
N5b6	R3b5			
N6b5	P5f1	**17.**	R8f1	M3b5
K4h5	R3f2		C7b1	M5f3
R6b6	R3h5		C9b1	K4f1
R6h5	P6h5		C7f1	K4h5
R5b1	K5b1		R8b2	S5f4

Red	Blue
C7b1	S4b5
C7b2	S5f4
C7b1	P5f1
R8b2	P3f1
C7f4	P8h7
C9b1	K5b1
R8f3	K5b1
C9f2	

18.

Red	Blue
R4h6	C1h4
R6f5	S5f4
C8h6	R3h4
C6f3	M5b7
R8b2	R5b5
N4f3	R5h7
N3b4	R7h6
P4f1	R4f1
R8b6	R4h6
K4h5	R6b1

19.

Red	Blue
fPf1	K6f1
R7f3	K6b1
C5h4	N5f6
P4h3*a	N6f5
N6f5*b	K6h5
N5f3	K5h6
P3h4	N5b6
N3b5	S4f5
R3f8	K6f1
P4h3	N6f5
N5b3	N5b7
N5f4	R4h6
R7h5	

a. | N6f7

Red	Blue
N5f4	N7b6
N6f5	S4f5
R3f8	K6f1
R7h5	

b. | S4f5

Red	Blue
P7h6	N5b6
R3f8	K6f1
P4h3	N6f5
N5f4	N5b6
N4f2	N6f5
N2f3	N5b7
N5b4	R4h6
R7h5	

20.

Red	Blue
C1f6	R8b6
C4h5	R8h9*a
N7f8*b	C6b2
C5f1	C6b1
fNf6*c	M1b3
N8f7	C6f4
N7f8	C6b4
N8b7	C6f4
(draw)	

a. N7f5   C6h4
(blue controls)

b. | R9f4

Red	Blue
C5f1	C6b2
fNf6	R9b4
N6b5	
(win)	

c. | R9f7

Red	Blue		Red	Blue
P4f1	K5h6		N6b4	C4h5
P3h4	K6h5		N4b6	K4h5
P4h5	K5h6		N6f7	K5f1
P5h4			C6h5	C5h6
(win)			N7b5	C6h5
			N5b7	C5h4
21. P5f1	S6b5		R4h5	K5h6
R2h5	K4b1		P2h3	K6b1
N9f8	N1f3		N7f6	
R5f1	K4f1			
N8b7	R4h3	**23.**	P5f1*a	K4h5
C5h6	C4h3		N1b3	K5h4
C1h6	C3h4		C1b1	K4b1
fCh8	C4h3		P8h7	K4b1
C8f2	K4f1		C1f2	S6f5
R5h6			N3f5	S5b6
			N5b4	S6f5
22. R4f9	K5f1		C3f2	
R4h5	K5b1			
N1b3	K5f1	**a.**		K4b1
N3b4	K5b1		N1b3	
N4f6	K5f1		(will win)	
N6f7	K5b1			
R5f2	K5h4	**24.**	C9f7	R2b3
R5h6	K4h5		P6f1	S5b4
P3h4	K5h6		R6f5	K5f1
R6f2	K6f1		R6h5	K5h6
N7b6	K6h5		R8h4	N8b6
N6b4	K5h6		C1h4	N6f4
C7h4	C1h6		N5f4*a	N4b6
R6b1	K6b1		N4f6*b	N6f4
N4f6	K6h5		N6f4	N4b6
R6h4	K5h4		R5b1	K6f1
C4h6	C6h4		N4f2	N6b7
R4f1	K4f1		C9b2	R2f2

Red	Blue		Red	Blue
N2b3		**26.**	R6f3	K5h4
			N9f8	K4h5
a.	N4f6		C6f6	M5b3
N4f3	K6f1		C6h1*a	M3f5
C9b2	M5f7		R2f5*b	S5b6
R5b2			R2b8*c	M5b7
			N8b6*d	K5f1
b.	N6b4		R2f7	K5f1
N6f4	N4b6		C1b2	S6b5
N4f2			R2b1	S5f6
			R2h4	K5b1
25.	R4f1	K4f1	N6f7	K5h4
P5f1	S6b5		R4h6	
N2f4	S5f6			
R1h2	S6b5	**a.**		S5b4
R2h5	K4h5		R2f5	K5f1
N6b4	K5f1		C9b1	K5f1
N4b6	K5b1		C1b2	R8b6
N6f7	K5f1		R2h5	S4f5
R4h5	K5h6		R5b1	
P2h3	R7b4			
R5h4	K6h5	**b.**		M5b7
N7f6	K5b1		R2h3	S5b6
R4b1	K5b1		R3h4	K5f1
C9f9	M1b3		C9b1	K5f1
N6b7	M3f5		R4b2	
R4h5	K5h6			
N7f6	M5b3	**c.**		S6f5
N6b4	M3f5		R2f8	S5b6
N4f2	R7b2		N8b6	K5h4
R5h6	C9b9		N6f7	K4f1
C9h3	C9h7		R2b1	S6f5
N2b3	C7f1		N7b8	
N3b1	P3h4			
R6b7	P5h4	**d.**		K5h4
K6f1				

Red	Blue		Red	Blue
N6f7	K4f1		P6f1	K5h6
R2f7	S6b5		P6h5	C5b7
R2h5	S6f5		N6b4	S5f6
N7b8	K4f1		N4f2	S6b5
C9b2			C6f7	S5b4
			N2b4	

27.

	Red	Blue			Red	Blue
	C1f5	S6f5				
	P4f1	K5h6	**a.**			K5h6
	N7f6	M5b3			C5h4	S6b5
	N6b4*ᵃ	M3f5			N6f4	S5f6
	N4f2	M5b7			N4f6	
	fNb3	K6f1				
	N3b5	K6f1	**b.**			C5b7
	N5b3	K6b1			N6b4	S5f6
	N3f2	K6f1			N4b2	S6b5
	C1b2	M7f9			N2f3	K6f1
	C8b2				P6h5	K6f1
					N3b4	

	Red	Blue
a.		K6f1
	N2f3	K6f1
	N3f2	K6b1
	C1b1	

29.

	Red	Blue
	N9f8	M5b3
	N8b7*ᵃ	M3f5
	N6f7	K5h4
	N7b5	K4f1
	P4h5	S6f5
	C4f8*ᶜ	S5f4
	N5f4	K4h5
	P5f1	K5f1
	C4h8*ᵈ	K5h6
	N4b6	S4b5
	C8b1	K6b1
	N6b5	K6b1
	N7f6	

28.

	Red	Blue
	fPh7	K4f1
	P8h7	K4f1
	N5f7	K4h5
	N7b5	K5h4
	N5f4	K4h5
	N4b6	K5b1
	rPh6*ᵃ	K5b1
	P7h6	K5h6
	C5h4	S6b5
	N6f4	S5f6
	N4f6	S6b5
	fPh5*ᵇ	K6h5

	Red	Blue
a.		M3f1
	N6f7	K5h4

	Red	Blue			Red	Blue
	fNb9*b	K4f1			N3f2	
	N9f8	K4f1				
	C9b2			c.		N5f7
					N6b4	K5h6
b.		K4h5			C5h4	
	N7f8	S5b4				
	N9f7			31.	C9f3	S4f5
					R6f1	K5h4
c.		S5f6			N5f7	K4h5
	N5f4	K4f1			N7f8	R4b5
	C9b2				R6f6	S5b4
					N8b9	S4f5
d.		K5b1			C6f7	C2b9
	N4b6	K5h4			M5f3*a	C2h3
	C9b1				C6b3	C3f2
					N9f8	C3b2
30.	P6f1	K5h6			C6h1*c	K5h4
	P6h5	K6f1			N8b7	C3f1
	N1b2	K6f1			C1f3	K4f1
	N7b6*a	N3b5			N3b5	K4f1
	N2b3*b	K6h5			C9b2	
	C8h5*c	N5b7				
	N3f5	K5h6		a.		R4b7
	N5f3	K6b1			N9f8*b	R4h1
	N3b5	K6f1			C6b3	R1b1
	N5b3	K6h5			C6h1	
	N6b4				(will win)	
a.		K6h5		b.		R4b1
	N6b4	K5h6			N3b4	P3h4
	C8h4				N4f2	
					(will win)	
b.		K6b1				
	N3f5	K6f1		c.		R4f1
	N5b3	K6b1			K5h6	S5f6

Red	Blue		Red	Blue
C1f3	K5f1	**33.**	R1f4	M5b7
C1h7*d	P7h6		R1h3	S5b6
N8b7	K5h6		N3f4	K5f1
N3f2			N4b6	K5h4
			R2f3	S4f5
d.		rPh4	N6f4	K4f1
N8b7	K5h4		N4b5	K4b1
N3f4	K4f1		N5f7	K4b1
C9b2			R3h4	S5b6
			N7f5	K4h5
32.	C2f6	R6h8	N5f7	K5h4
K5h6	C9f7		N7f9	N3f4
C3b2	C9f2		R2h7*a	P2h3
R1b3	P5h6		R7b4	fNb3
M3f5	P4f1		M5f7	K4h5
M5f3*a	R8h6		N9b7	K5f1
C3h2	R6h8		N7b6	K5h6
R1h4	R8h9		N6b4	N4f5
M3b1*b	R9h5		N4b5	N5f4
R4f8	R5h8		N5b3	N4f6
R4h3	P5h4		M7b5	K6h5
K6h5	rPh5		N3f4	N6b5
P5h6	K4h5		N4b3	N5f6
R3h5	K5h6		N3f4	
R5b6			(draw)	
a.		P4f1	**a.**		rNf5
C3h6	P5h4		R7f1	K4f1
K6h5	R8h6		R7b7	N5f6
R1f3			N9b8	K4h5
			N8f7	K5b1
b.		R9h8	N7b6	K5f1
C2h3	R8h7		N6b4	K5h6
R4f4			N4f2	K6h5
			N2b3	N6b7

Red	Blue
R7h6	N7f6
R6f1	N6f7
M5b7	
(will win)	

34.

Red	Blue
C3f9	M9b7
P6f1	K5h4
N7f8	K4f1
C1f3	S5f4
P2f1	S6f5
N8b7	K4b1
C1f1*a	S5b6
N7f5	K4h5
N5f4	K5h4
R5f6*b	K4f1
R5h8	K4h5
C1b1	

a.

Red	Blue
	M7f5
P2f1	S5b6
N7f5	K4h5
N5f4	K5h4
N4b2	K4f1
N2b4	

b.

Red	Blue
	K4h5
N4b3	M7f5
P2f1	

35.

Red	Blue
N9f8	N3b2
C1h6	R4f1
fRf1	K4b1
P4h5	K4h5
fRf1	K5b1
fRf1	K5f1

Red	Blue
R1f5	K5f1
rRh6*a	P5h6*b
K4h5	R4h6
R1b2	R6b3
R1f1	R6h8
R1h5	K5h6
R6b2	
(win)	

a.

Red	Blue
	R4f4
R6b8	P6f1
R1h5	K5h6
R5h4	K6h5
R4b7	C7h6
R4h2	C2b4
R2f5	rPh6
R2h4	K5h6
R6f3	
(will win)	

b.

Red	Blue
K4f1	P6f1
K4h5	P5f1
M3f5	P6h5
K5b1	P5f1
K5h4	R4h6
(win)	

36.

Red	Blue
fRh5	S6f5
R8h2	S5b6
R2f3*a	C2h6
C9h3*c	R7b2
C3f3*d	R7b4
R2h3	C6b2
P4f1	K5h4
P4h5	K4f1

	Red	Blue			Red	Blue
	R3b1	K4f1			R3h5	K5h6
	R3b6	K4b1			R6h4	K6f1
	R3h6	K4h5			N7f6	K6b1
	N3f1	P1h2			R5h4	K6h5
	N1f3*e	C6h1			N6b5	S4b5
	R6h9	P2h3			N5f7	K5h4
	N3b5	P4h5			R4h6	S5f4
	R9b1				C5h6	S4b5
					N5f6	S5f4*b
a.		K5h4			N6f7	S4b5
	R2h4	K4f1			fNb6	S5f4
	C9h3*b	R7b2			N6f4	S4b5
	R4h5				N7b6	S5f4
					N6f8	S4b5
b.		M5f7			N8f7	
	C3f2	K4f1				
	R4h7			**a.**		K5h6
					R3h4	S5f6
c.		M5f7			R6f1	K6f1
	C3f3	S6f5			C5h4	S6b5
	C3b6	S5b6			N5f4	S5f6
	N3f4				N4f3	
d.		S6f5		**b.**	N6f4	S4b5
	C3b2	S5b6			N4f6	S5f4
	P4f1	K5h4			N6f4	S4b5
	P4h5	K4f1			N7b6	S5f4
	R2b1				N6b8	S4f5
					N8f7	
e.		C6f2				
	R6h4	P4f1		**38.**	C8f5	S4f5
	R4f6	K5b1			P4h5	K5h6
	N3b5				N7f6	R3b7
					C1h4	R3h2
37.	C1h5*a	S5f4			N6b4	N8b6

Red	Blue		Red	Blue
N4b5	N6b5		R3b3	P5f1
N5f3	N5b7		R3f2	R6b5
N3b4	N7f6		C1b1	
N4f6	N6b5		(will win)	
N6f4	N5f6			
N4f6	K6h5	**b.**		K5h4
N6f8	N6f4		R3h6	K4h5
C4h7	N4f5		R6h7	R6h4
C7b2	N5b7		R7h5	K5h6
C7f2	N7f5		R5h4	K6h5
C7b2	N5b7		R4b7	R4h8
			R4f4	K5h4
39. R1h5	K5h6		R4f2	M7b5
C1f4	K6f1		R4f1	M5f7
R5h4	K6h5		R4h7	
R4h6	K5h6		(will win)	
R6f1	M7b5			
R6f1	M5f7	**c.**		P5f1
R6h4	K6h5		R3h5	K5h4
R4h3	R3h6		R5h6	K4h5
K6h5*a,b	P5f1		K5h6	K5h6
M7f9*c	P3h4		R6h4	K6h5
R3h5	K5h4		R4b6	P6h5
R5h6	K4h5		C1b7	
R6b7	R6h2		(will win)	
M9b7	R2h8			
R6h4	R8f2	**40.** fCh6	R4f2
K5f1	R8b8		C2h6	R4h8*a
R4f3	R8f7		N6f5	R8f1
K5b1	R8h4		C6f1	fPf1
R4h5	K5h4		K6h5	P6h5
R5f1			K5h6	fPh4
(will win)			K6h5	P5f1
			K5h4	R8h6
a.	P3f1		N5b4	C1b5

Red	Blue		Red	Blue
C6h1	P4f1*c		(will win)	
R5b7	C1f7			
R5b1	P4h5	**c.**	R2f6	R6b4
K4h5	R6h4*d,e,i		R5b7	C1f7
C1b4	R4f3		R5b1	R6h8
K5f1	P3f1*k		(will win)	
R2b1	C1b1			
K5f1	R4b5	**d.**	R2f1	R4f3
R2f3	C1h6*l,m		K5f1	P3f1
C1h5	P3h4*o		R2h9	P3h4
C5h6	P4f1		K5f1	R4h5
R2h5	C6f1		K5h4	R5h7
P3f1	C6h5		(will win)	
R5h9	R4h5			
K5h4	C5h6	**e.**	R2f6	K4b1
R9f4	K4b1		R2h9	R4f3
P3h4	C6b7		K5f1	P3f1*f,g
R9h4	K4h5		C1h5	P3h4
K4b1	P4h5		K5f1	R4h7*h
R4b4	R5f4		C5h4	R7h5
K4f1	P5h6		K5h4	K4h5
	(will win)		R9b5	R5h7
			(will win)	
a.	N6f7*b	fPh4		
K6f1	P3f1	**f.**	C1b3	P3h4
K6b1	P3f1		K5f1	R4h5
K6f1	R8f1		K5h4	K4h5
R2f2	P6h5		N4f2	R5b4
	(win)		N2f4	P4h5
			R9b4	C1h7
b.		R8f1	C1h3	R5h7
R2f2	fPh4		R9h5	K5h6
K6h5	P5f1		(will win)	
R5b7	P4h5			
K5h6		**g.**	R9b3	P3h4

Red	Blue
K5f1	R4h5
K5h4	R5h7
N4f6	C1h3
N6f8	R7b2
K4b1	R7f1
K4f1	P4h5
	(will win)

h.

Red	Blue
R9h4	C1b2
C5h4	R7h5
K5h4	K4h5
	(will win)

i.

Red	Blue
C1b3	R4f3
K5f1	P3f1*j
K5f1	R4h5
K5h4	K4h5
N4b6	R5b5
R2f6	K5b1
R2h4	P3h4
K4b1	C1b1
N6f8	P4h5
	(will win)

j.

Red	Blue
P3h4	R4h2
R2f6	K4b1
C1f1	P3h4
K5f1	C1b2
	(will win)

k.

Red	Blue
C1h9	P3h4
K5f1	R4h5
K5h4	K4h5
R2f6	K5b1
N4f2	R5b2

Red	Blue
K4b1	P4h5
	(will win)

l.

Red	Blue
K5b1	P3h4
K5b1	R4h5
K5h4	P4h5
R2h6	K4h5
C1f3	C6b8
	(will win)

m.

Red	Blue
R2h5	C6f1
P3f1	C6h5*n
R5h4	P3h4
C1f2	R4h5
K5h4	C5h6
R4h9	K4h5
	(will win)

n.

Red	Blue
R5h9	P3h4
C1f2	R4h5
K5h4	P4h5
R9h4	R5h7
	(will win)

o.

Red	Blue
K5h4	C6f1
R2h5	P4h5
P3f1	R4f3
R5b1	R4f1
C5h6	R4h2
	(will win)

41.

Red	Blue
——*a	
N2b4	R5f1*b
R6h5	R5f4
N4b5	K5f1

	Red	Blue		Red	Blue
	P1f1			N7f8	K4f1
	(draw)			R8h6	S5f4
				C5h6	S4b5
a.	N2f4	K5f1		N8b6	K4f1
	S4f5	R5b1		C6b5	
	K6b1	R5f5			
	K6f1	R5b5	**45.**	R9h6	S5b4
	N4f3	K5b1		R8f7	S6f5
		(will win)		C4f7	N8f7
				C4h6	
b.	N4b5	R5f1			
	K6b1	R5f1	**46.**	C8b3	N6f4
		(will win)		C8h6	N4b3
				P8h7	N3f2
42.	P6f1	N3f4		C6f8	N2f1
	P2h3	N9b7		fPh6	K5b1
	P3h4	N7b6		C6h7	N1b2
	K5h4	P7f1		C7h6	N2f1
	K4f1	fPh5		C6h7	
	K4f1	P4h5			
	K4h5	N6b8	**47.**	C3f3	M5b7
	P8h7	N8f7		R6f8	K5h4
	P7h6	N7b5		R9f3	K4f1
				N3b5	M7f5
43.	R7h6	P5h6		R9b1	K4f1
	K4h5	fPh5		N5b3	M5f7
	K5h6	P4f1		R9b6	R8h9
	R6b6	P5h4		R9h1	R9h6
	K6f1	M1b3		K4h5	R6h5
	K6f1			K5h4	K4h5
				R1h5	R5f1
44.	R7f1	K4f1		M3f5	
	N8b7	K4f1			
	R7b2	K4b1	**48.**	P4h5	K5f1
	R7h8	K4b1		P7h6	K5b1

Red	Blue
P6f1	K5h6
N3b4	P2h3
M7b9	M5f7
M1b3	

49.

Red	Blue
R6f1*a	R1f1
R6b1	R7h6
R4b8	R1h4
K5h6	N7f6
S5b4	

(draw)

a.

Red	Blue
	R1h4
N5f3*b	R4h5
K5h6	R5h4
K6f1	N7f6
K6f1	R7b8
R4h3	N1f2
R3b8	

(will win)

b.

Red	Blue
	N7f6
R4h5	K5h6
R5f1	K6f1
C1f4	K6f1
R5b2	

(win)

50.

Red	Blue
fCh4	rPh6
P4f1	K6f1
P3f1	K6b1
P3f1	M5b7
R3f9	K6f1
C1h4	P5h6
R3h5	R6h5

Red	Blue
R5b8	P4h5
K5f1	P3h4
R1f8	K6f1
R1b1	K6b1
R1h5	

(will win)

51.

Red	Blue
P3f1	K6f1
R6h4	C9h6
R4f4	S5f6
C1h4	R8h6
C4f3	M3b1
P3h2*a,b	M1b3
P7f1	M3f5*c
P2h3	R6f1
N6b4	M5f3

(draw)

a.

Red	Blue
	K6b1
N6f5	R6f1
N5b3	K6h5
N3b4	

(win)

b.

Red	Blue
	P5h6
K6f1	P6h7
K6f1	P7h6
K6h5	P6h7
C4b3	R6f3
N6f7	M1b3
P7f1	M3f5
N7b6	M5f7
P2h3	M7b9
P3h2	K6b1
P7f1	P7h6

	Red	Blue			Red	Blue
	P7f1	P6h7			P6h5	K5f1
	P7h6	P7h6			R9b1	K5f1
	P6f1	P6h7			R9h4	K5h4
	P6h5	P7h6			N3b4	K4h5*a
	N6f4				N4b6	K5h4
	(will win)				R4h8*b	P4h3
					R8b2*c	K4b1
c.	P7f1	K6b1			R8h6	K4h5
	P7f1	K6h5			R6h3	M7f5
		(win)			R3h2*d	K5h4
					R2h6	K4h5
52.	P1f1	P5f1			N6f4	K5h6
	P1h2	P5f1			R6f2	K6f1
	P2f1	P5f1			N4b3	M5f7
	P9f1	P5f1			N3f5	K6h5
	P9h8	K5f1			N5f3	K5h6
	P8f1	K5b1			R6h4	
	P2h3	K5f1			(win)	
	P8h7	K5b1				
	P3h4	K5f1	a.	R4h6	K5h6
	P7h6	K5b1		N4b3	R5b1
	P4f1	K5f1		R6b5	R5b2
	P6f1	M5f7		R6h4	K6h5
	K5h4	P5h6		R4h5	R5f1
	P4h3	M7b5		N3b5	
	K4h5	P6h5			(draw)	
		(draw)				
(In this example, if blue moves			b.		R5b1
first then red will win.)				N6f4	R5b4
				R8b2	P4f1
53.	C3f2	M5b7		R8h6	
	R2h6	R5h6		(win)	
	N2f3	R6b5			
	R6h9	S5b4	c.		P6f1
	R9f2	S6f5		R8h6	K4h5

144 · ANSWERS TO EXERCISES

Red	Blue		Red	Blue
R6h3	K5h4		P3h4	R8h7
R3h6	K4h5		N6b4	
R6f3	K5b1			
N6f7	K5h6	**55.**	fCh4	R6f1
N7b5	K6f1		C1h4	R6h7*[a]
R6h4	K6h5		R1h4*[c]	P6h5
R4h5	K5h6		K5h4	N2f4
N5b3	K6b1		C4h7	N4f6
N3f2	K6f1		C7f5	C5f7
N2f3	K6b1		P6f1	
N3b2	K6f1		(win)	
R5h4	K6h5			
R4b9	R5h7	**a.**	P5f1	K6f1
R4f3	P3f1		R1f6	K6f1
R4h5	K5h6		R3f2	P4h5
K6h5	P3f1		K5h6	R2h4
M5f3			R1h6	N2b4
(win)			C4h5*[b]	P3f1
			R3h6	
d.	M5b3			(will win)
N6f4	K5h6			
N4f6	K6h5	**b.**		fPh4
R8f2	K5f1		C5b3	P6h5
N6b5	P3h4		R3f2	K6b1
R2h6	P6f1		R3f1	K6f1
N5f3			R3h6	P4f1
(win)			R6b7	P5h4
			K6f1	
54.	P6h5	S6f5		(draw)
P4h5	K5h4			
N7b6	C1h4	**c.**		P4h5
N6b8	C4h1		K5h6	R2h4
N8b6	C1h4		C4h6	
N6b7	C4h1		(win)	
N7b6	C1h4			

	Red	Blue			Red	Blue
56.	R2f4	M5b7		**58.**	R7f2	K4f1
	R2h3	S5b6			N7b5	K4b1*a
	M3b5	R7b9			P4h5*b	S6f5
	P6f1	K4h5			N5f7	K4f1
	C1h9	R3h4			R7b2	K4b1
	K6f1	C5h1			R7h2	K4b1
	N8b7	S6f5			R2f2	S5b6
	C9h8	R7f3			R2h4	
	P6f1	K5h6			(win)	
	C8h4	R7h6				
	N7f5*a	C1h6		**a.**	N5f7	K4f1
	N5b4	C6b6			R7b2	K4b1
	C4f2				R7h8	K4b1
					N7f8	K4f1
a.		R6f1			R8h6	S5f4
	N5b3				C7h6	S4b5
					C6b3	S5f4
					S6b5	S4b5
57.	P4h5	K5h4			C6b1	R2b8
	P5f1	K4h5			C6h9	
	R3h5	K5h4			(draw)	
	P7f1	K4b1				
	R5h6	S5f4		**b.**		K4h5
	P7h6	K4h5			R7b1	K5b1
	R6h5	M3f5			N5f4	K5h4
	R5f1	M7f5			R7h6	
	C1h5	M5f3			(win)	
	C5b5	M3b5				
	M5f3	M5f3		**59.**	rRh6	R4b4
	M3b5	M3b5			R1h6	K4h5
	M5f7	M5f7			R6b1	R2h4*a
	M7b5	M7b5			R6b4	C2f3
	M5b7	M5b7			R6b1	P5f1
	M7f5	M7f5			C1b3*b	P6h5
	M5b3	M5b3			K5h4	rPh6
	C5h2	M3f1				

Red	Blue		Red	Blue
C1f8	M7f9		P5f1	K6h5
C1h4	P6f1		P3h2	
C4b8	P5h6		(draw)	
K4f1	C2h4			
P7h6	C4h5	**a.**	R7b2	C3f2
P4f1			R7b5	R7f1
(win)			K4f1	P5f1
			S6f5	R7h3*b
a. R6f4	R4b8		P1h2	M7b5
C1f5	M7f9		rPh3	R3b5
C1h6	C2f3		P8h7	R3b4
M7f5	P5f1		P3h4	R3f4
K5h6	P5h4		P4h5	R3h6
P7h6	C2b8		S5f4	R6b3
C6b7	C2h6		P5f1	R6h5
K6f1			P6h5	K5f1
(draw)			(draw)	
b.	C2h4	**b.**	P2h3	R3b7
P7h6	P6h5			(will win)
K5h6	rPh4			
C1f8	M7f9	**61.**	R1h4*a	P5f1
P6h5	K5h4		R4h5	R5f8
P4f1	M9b7		K5h4	K6h5
P4h5			P4f1	R5f1
(win)			K4f1	P4h5
			K4f1	R5h7
60. R7b1	M5f3*a		P4f1	
R7f2	C3b7			
P8h7	P5h6	**a.**		P5h6
S5f4	R7h4		K5h4	P6f1
P7h6	K5h6		K4f1	R5f7
rPh5	R4b8		P4f1	K6h5
P1h2	M3b5		P4f1	
rPh3	R4h5			

	Red	Blue			Red	Blue
62.	N7f5	K4b1			R3f5	
	N3f4	S5b6			(win)	
	N5f7	K4b1		**c.**		M9b7
	C2f2	S6f5			R6f5	K4h5
	P4f1	M5b7			R6f2	K5f1
	P4h3	S5b6			R6b1	K5b1
	P3h4	C5b6			R6h3	P7h6
	P4h5	K4h5			R3b8	
	C2b8	P3h4			(draw)	
	S5b6	C3h8				
				64.	R1f5	S5b6
63.	R1h4	P5h6			R2f6	S6f5
	K4h5	K5h4*a			P4f1	K5h6
	N8f6*b	M7f9			C2b7	K6f1
	R3f1	P4h5			rRh4	C5h6
	K5h6	fPh7			C2h8	rPh4
	R4b6	S5f4			R1b1	K6b1
	R4h6*c	P7h6			R4f4	S5f6
	R6f5	K6h5			R1h6*a	P1h2
	R6h5	K5h6			C8f7	M3f1
	R5h1	P9h8			R6b1	S6b5
	R1b1	P8h7			R6f2	K6f1
	R1h4	K6h5			R6b7	P2h3
	R4b5	P5h6			C8b1	S5f6
	K6f1				C8h7	P3h4
	(draw)				R6b1	P5h4
					K6f1	
a.	N8b6	P6h5			(draw)	
	K5h4	P4f1				
		(will win)		**a.**		P4h3
					C8f7	M3f1*b
b.		K4f1			R6f1	K6f1
	R3f3	fPh5			R6h5	P5h6
	K5h4	P4f1			R5h1	P6h5
	R4h5	K4h5			R1b8	

Red	Blue		Red	Blue
(win)			P2h3	P7h6
			P3h4	K5h6
b. R6b1	K6f1		R6b4	
R6f1	K6b1		(win)	
R6b1	S6b5*c			
R6h5		**b.**	R6b7	P8h7
(win)			M5b3	P5h4
			K4f1	P7h6
c. R6f2	K6f1		(win)	
R6b8	P5h4			
K6f1	P1h2	**c.**		P3f1
C8b1	S5f6		R6h4	P4f1
C8h7			R4h5	K5h4
	(draw)		R5h6	R4h5
			R6b3	P7f1
65. R1f2	M5b7		R6h8	P7f1
R3f2	N6b7		R8f1	
R1h3	K5f1		(win)	
R3b1*a	K5b1			
R3h6	P7f1*b	**d.**	P7f1	
R6b5*c	P7h6*d			(draw)
P2h3	P3f1			
P3h4	P4f1	**e.**		K5h6
R6b3	P6f1		P9h8	rPh4
R6h5	P8h7		K5b1	P4h3
M5b3	P5f1		P8h7	P3h4
K4f1	P6h5		P7h6	P4h5
K4h5*e	fPh6		K5h4	P5h6
M3f1	K5h4		M3f5	P6f1
P4h5	K4f1		M5b7	P3f1
M1f3			K4h5	P6h5
	(draw)		M7f5	
			(win)	
a.	K5f1			
R3h6	P7f1	**66.**	N1f3	K5h4

Red	Blue
N3f4*a	K4h5
N4f6	K5h4
P8h7	K4b1
N6b8	N5f3
P7f1	K4h5
P7h6*b	K5f1*c
N8b7	K5h4
C9f1*d	R5f1
K4h5	S6b5
C9h5	fPh5
K5h4	rPh6
C5b8	P4f1
N7b5	K4b1
N5b6	P4h5
N6b4	

(draw)

a.

Red	Blue
	S6b5
C9b1	K4b1
N4b5	K4b1
N5f7	K4f1
N7f8	K4b1
C9f2	

(win)

b.

Red	Blue
	K5b1
P6f1	K5h6
N8b6	

(win)

c.

Red	Blue
C9f1	R5f1
K4h5	P5f1

(will win)

d.

Red	Blue
	S6b5

Red	Blue
N7f8	K4h5
C9h5	

(will win)

67.

Red	Blue
rCh4	R6b2
C1h4	N5b6
P4f1	K6f1
P6h5	R5f1
R3f8	K6b1
R1f8	M5b7
R3h5	M3f5
R5h8	P4h5
K5f1	N6f4
K5h6	R6f2
K6f1	R6b1
K6b1	N4f2
R8b6	R6h2
R1b1	P8h7*a
P2h3*c	P7h6
P3f1	R2h6
R1b2	K6h5
R1h6*e	M5f7
R6h5	M7b5
R5h6	M5f7
R6h5	M7b5
R5h6	

(draw)

a.

Red	Blue
R1h6	P7h6
R6f1	K6f1
P2h3	K6h5*b
R6b3	R2h5

(will win)

b.

Red	Blue
P3h4	M5b3

Red	Blue
R6b3	R2h5
	(will win)

c.		K6h5
	P3h4	M5f7
	P4f1	R2h5
	R1h3*d	R5f1
	K6b1	M7b9
	P4h5	R5b7
	R3b7	
	(draw)	

d.		M7f9
	R3h2	
	(win)	

e.		R6h5
	P3h4	
	(win)	

	Red	Blue
68.	R1h7	N7f6
	K5h4	C6b3
	R7f4	M1b3
	R1h5	N6b8
	K4h5	N8b7
	K5h4	N7b5
	C1h5	N5b4
	rPh3	N4b5
	C5f5	K6h5
	P3h4	C6h2
	C5h8*a	K5h4
	P9f1	K4f1
	P9f1	C2f5
	P9f1	P5h6
	C8b4	P4h5

Red	Blue
C8h1	C2f1
C1f4	K4f1
P4h3	M5f3
C1b7	K4h5
C1h5	P6h5
P9h8	
(draw)	

a.		M5f7
	P2h3	C2h6
	C8f1	M3f1
	P3h4	K5h4
	rPh5	C6h5
	P4h5	C5b3
	C8h5	
	(will win)	

	Red	Blue
69.	N4f6	K5f1
	M3b5	rPf1
	N3b5	N5f3
	N6f7	K5h4
	N7b9	K4b1
	N9b7	K4b1
	N7f8	K4h5
	S6b5	P7h6
	S5f4	P8h7
	N8b7	P7h6
	N7b5	fPh5
	K6h5	rPh4
	N5b6	P3h4
	M5f3	P6h7
	K5h4	
	(will win)	

	Red	Blue
70.	N4f6	K5h6

Red	Blue
C5b1	S5f6
R6h4	R5f1
K6f1	S4f5
P7h6*a	R5b2
P6h5	R5h3
R4b1	R3h6
P3h4	

	Red	Blue
a.		R1h2
	P3h4*b	K6h5
	P4h5	S6b5
	P6h5	K5h4
	R4f6	

	Red	Blue
b.		K6f1
	P6h5	

	Red	Blue
71.	fPf1	M5b7
	P2h3	K6f1
	R1f4	K6f1
	R1f4	M7b9
	R1b1	K6b1
	R1f1	K6f1
	P3f1	K6h5
	C1f5	R6b6
	C1h4	K5h4
	C4f2	P4f1
	K5f1	N5b7*a
	P6h5	R5h3
	R1h4	K4h5
	C4h5	
	(win)	

	Red	Blue
a.	R1h5	R5f1
	P6h5*b	N7b6

Red	Blue
P3h4	N6b8
P4h3	K4h5
P5h4	P3f1
rPh2	P3f1
P2h1	P3h4
C4h2	K5h4
P4h5	K4h5
P5h6	K5h4
(draw)	

	Red	Blue
b.		P5h4*c
	P3h4	rPh5
	C4h5	N7b6
	P3h2	P3f1
	P2h1	P3f1
	C5h2	P3h4
	C2b2	N6b5
	C2h5	
	(win)	

	Red	Blue
c.	C4h6	rPh5
	C6h5	N7b6
	rPh4	P3f1*d
	P3h2	P3f1
	P2h1	P3h4
	C5h2	
	(win)	

	Red	Blue
d.	M3f5	P5h4
	M5b7	P3f1
	M7f9	P3f1
	P4h5	N6b5
	C5b2	P4h5
	C5b2	
	(draw)	

	Red	Blue			Red	Blue
72.	C5f5	R1h5	**c.**			P8f1
	P4f1	K5h6			M5b3	P3h4
	R6h9	R5f1			R6b1	P5h4
	R9f1	S5b4			K4f1	
	R9h6	R5b3			(win)	
	P3f1	K6f1				
	R6h5	P9h8	**d.**			P7h8
	R5h6	K6h5*a			P3h4	S6b5
	M7b5	P4h3*b			K4f1	P8h7
	R6b7*c	P3h4			K4h5	
	R6b1	P5h4			(win)	
	K4f1	P8h7				
	P3f1	K5h6	**73.**		N2f3	K5h6
	P7f1	P7h8			C1h4	S5f6
	M5f3	P8h7			N4b3	S6b5
	P3f1*d	K6h5			rNb4	S5f6
	M3b5	K5h6			N4f2	S6b5
	P3h4	S6b5			N2f4	S5f6
	M5f3	S5b4			N4f5	S6b5
	(draw)				N5b4	S5f6
					N4f6	S6b5
a.	R6b7	P5f1			N6f4	S5f6
	K4f1	P4h5			N4f6	S6b5
	K4f1	P8h7			N3b4	S5f6
	(win)				N4b6	S6b5
					rNb4	S5f6
b.	R6b4	P8h7			N4f3	S6b5
	R6h5	K5h4			N3f4	S5f6
	M5b3	P3h4			N4f6	S6b5
	R5h6	K4h5			fNb4	S5f6
	R6b4	P5h4			N4b2	S6b5
	K4f1	P4h5			N2b4	S5f6
	K4b1	P7h6			N4b3	S6b5
	(win)				N3b4	S5f6
					N4b6	S6b5

	Red	Blue
	R7f8	

	Red	Blue
b.	R5f5	K4f1
	C9f1	rPh8
	C9h6	R4h6
	C6h4*c	R6b1
	R5b5	K4b1
	(draw)	

74.

Red	Blue
fRf3	S5b4
rRh5	S6f5
R5f4	K5f1
R7b1	K5b1
C1f7	M7f5
N4f6	K5h6
P2f1	N8b9
P2h3	M5b7
R7h4	R6b1
C2f7	

	Red	Blue
c.		P2h3
	R5b3	R6h4
	C4h7	
	(win)	

75.

Red	Blue
R2f5	M5b7
R2h3	S5b6
C3h9*a	R1b1
R3b9	R1h4
K6h5	R4b5
R3f4	R4h5
K5h4	R5h2
R3h6	K4h5
R6h5	K5h4
K4h5	R2h4*b
R5h9	R4h5
K5h4	K4h5
R9h4	S6f5
(draw)	

76.

Red	Blue
fCh4	R6f1
C3h4	R6h7
C4b4	R7f2
P3f1	P5h4
K6h5	rPh5
K5h4	P5f1
P5f1*a	K6h5
C4h6	P8h7
C6h8	P7h6
M7f5	P5h6
K4h5	rPh5*b,c
P6f1	K5f1
P7h6	K5h6
P2h3	K6f1
C8f6	P6h5
K5h6	rPh4
C8h6	P4h3
C6h7	P3h4
C7h6	P4h3
C6h7	P3h4
(draw)	

	Red	Blue
a.		R7b9
	P6f1	K4h5
	P8f1	S6f5
	P6h5	K5h6
	C1f1	
	(win)	

	Red	Blue
a.		K6f1

Red	Blue
C4f6	P5f1
K4f1	P4h5
K4h5	K6f1
(will win)	
b. P7h6	K5h6
C8f6	P6h5
K5h6	rPh4
C8h6	P4h3
C6h7	M3b1
P6h7	P3h4
	(win)
c. P2h3	P6h5
K5h4	rPh6
	(win)
77. fRf1	K5f1
R4f4	K5f1
fRh5	K5h4
R5h3*a	R5f1
C9h5*b	P1f1
P1f1	P1h2
P1f1	P2h3
P1h2*d	P3f1
R3b2	R5b5
R3h5	K4h5
C5b7	R8h5
P2h3	P3f1
P3f1	P3h4
P3h4	K5h4
R4h7	P4f1
R7b1	K4b1
P4h5	
(win)	

	Red	Blue
a.		R8b2
	R3b2	R5b4
	R3b6	R5f5
	R4b1	K4b1
	R3f7	K4b1
	R3f1	K4f1
	R4f1	K4f1
	C9h5	
	(win)	
b.		P5h6
	R4b7	R8h6
	K4f1	R5b6*c
	R3h9	
	(win)	
c.	R3b2	K4b1
	R3b2	R5f4
	P1f1	K4h5
	R3h4	P1f1
	P1h2	P1h2
	P2f1	P2h3
	P2h3	P3h4
	P3f1	P4f1
	M1f3	P4f1
	R4b3	R5f3
	K4b1	P4f1
	R4h5	R5b1
	M3b5	
	(draw)	
d.		R8b5
	C5b7	R5f1
	R3b2	R5b6
	R3f1	

	Red	Blue		Red	Blue
	(win)			R2f8	R7h6
				R2h4	R5h6
78.	——*a			R4b6	R6f7
	rCh6	R4f4		K4h5	R6h5
	C2h6	R4h5*c		K5h4	P3h4
	K5h6	R5h7		R5h4	P4f1
	R2f9	R7b7		C6f3	R5h4
	R2h3	R7b8*e		C6h5	R4b5
	K6h5	R7f9		C5f1	K4h5
	K5f1	R7b4		K4f1	P5f1
	C6b4	R7h5		C5h9	P5f1
	K5h4	R5f4		C9b8	P5f1
	C6f1	R5h4		R4b6	P4f1
	C6h5*f	R4b4		C9f9	R4f6
	C5b1	R4h5		K4b1	R4h5
	C5h6*h	P5f1			(win)
	R5h7	R5f4			
	R7b6	R5h4	d.	R5h4	R5h4
	R7h5	R4b5		C6h5	P3f1
	K4h5			R2f3	P3h4
	(draw)			R2h9	R7f9
				K4f1	P4h5
a.	fCh6	R4f2		K4h5	R7b1
	C2h6	R4h5*b		R4b7	R4f1
	K5h4	R7b8			(win)
	C6h4	R5h4			
	R5b2	R7f8	e.	R5b2	R7f5
	R5f2	R4f4		C6b1	R7f1
	R5b8	R4b1		C6f3	P3h4
		(win)		K6h5	P4f1
				K5h4	P4h5
b.	K5h6	R7h4			(win)
		(win)			
			f.		R4b5
c.	K5h4	R7b8*d		C5b1	R4h5

Red	Blue
C5h6	R5h6
K4h5*g	P5f1
R5h7	P3h2
R7b3	K4h5
C6h5	K5h6
R7h5	R6f4
K5f1	P2h3
C5h9	R6f1
K5b1	P3h4
R5b1	R6b1
K5b1	P4f1
R5f1	
(draw)	

g.

Red	Blue
	R6f5
C6f6	R6h4
R5b2	P3f1
C6h9	P3h4
K5h4	R4h9
C9h8	R9b4
K4f1	R9h6
K4h5	R6h4
C8h6	
(draw)	

h.

Red	Blue
	P3f1
R5h7	P3h2
R7b2	P5f1
R7h6	K4h5
R6h5	K5h4
C6h1*i	P2h3
C1f1	P3f1
C1f8	R5h6
K4h5	P5f1
C1h5	P3h4

Red	Blue
C5b5	R6f4
(draw)	

i.

Red	Blue
	R5h9
R5h6	K4h5
C1h5	R9h5
C5f1	
(will win)	

79. ——*a

Red	Blue
C2f6	R6h8
C3b2	P3h4
C3h6	P4h5*b
R1h3	P6h5
C6f7*c,d,k	R8h6
P5h4*o	R6h5
R3f1	R5h8
M1b3*p	M3b5
R3h6	
(win)	

a.

Red	Blue
C3f6	R6h7
C2f6	R7f9
M1b3	P3h4
K6h5	rPh5
(win)	

b.

Red	Blue
R1h5	R8f9
R5b3	R8h5
K6h5	
(draw)	

c.

Red	Blue
	rPf1
C6b6	
(will win)	

	Red	Blue		Red	Blue
d.		M3b5		(win)	
	P5h4	rPh4			
	M1b3	R8f9	**h.**		R8b5
	C6h5	P5h4		R4h1	K5h4
	K6f1	P4f1		R1h6	K4h5
	K6b1*e	P4f1		R6b2	R8h6
	K6h5	R8b1		R6f6	R6b2
	R3h6	K4h5		R6h5*i	M1f3
	R6h4*f,g,h	R8h7		R5b2	R6f1
	K5h4	K5h4		C5b2*j	R6f1
	C5f1	R7f1		C5h8	K5h6
	K4f1	R7b6		C8b4	M3b1
	P4h5	R7h4		C8h2	R6b1
	C5h1			C2f7	
	(win)			(win)	
e.		R8b2	**i.**		M1b3
	K6h5	R8h6		C5h6	K5h4
	C5h8			R5b1	R6f1
	(win)			C6h8	R6h4
				R5f3	K4f1
f.		K5h4		C8f1	M3f1
	C5f1	K4h5		C8h6	R4h3
	R4h1	P4h5		R5b3	
	K5h6	P5h4		(win)	
	K6h5	R8b8			
	R1h3	M1b3	**j.**		C5h6
	R3b2			R6h3	R5h6
	(win)			K5h4	C6h5
				R3h5	
g.		M1b3		(win)	
	K5h4	M5f7			
	R4h1	K5h4	**k.**		M3b5
	R1h6	K4h5		P5h4	M5f7
	R6f5			R3f2	rPh4

Red	Blue
M1b3	P4f1
R3h6*[l]	R8f8
C6b6	K4h5
C6h5	P5h4
R6b4	
(win)	

l.

Red	Blue
	K4h5
R6h5	K5h4
R5b4	R8h7
M3f1	R7f7
K6h5*[m]	P4h5
R5h8*[n]	K4f1
R8f7	K4f1
R8b1	K4b1
R8h5	
(win)	

m.

Red	Blue
	R7h5
C6h8	K4h5
R5f1	P4h5
M1f3	P5f1
K5h6	
(will win)	

n.

Red	Blue
	R7h9
C6b8	
(win)	

o.

Red	Blue
	R6h8
M1b3	
(win)	

p.

Red	Blue
	rPh4
R3h6	R8f8

Red	Blue
C6b5	K4h5
C6h5	P5h4
R6b3	R8h4
K6f1	M1b3
C5b3	M3f1
M3f5	M3b5
C5f7	
(will win)	

80.

Red	Blue
——*[a]	
R5f4	R7b1
K4b1	R7b2*[b]
S5f6	N5f3*[d,e]
rRh7	N3f4
R7f8	K6b1*[h]
R5f1	R7f3
K4f1	C6f2*[i,k]
R7b3	C6b3*[m,n]
R5b3	R7b5*[q]
K4b1	N4b5
R7h6	R7h6
K4h5	C6h5
R6f4	K6f1
R6b1	N5b4
R5f4	K6b1
R5h6	
(draw)	

a.

Red	Blue
R5f5	R7b1
K4b1	C6f5
S5f4	R7f1
(win)	

b.

Red	Blue
K4f1	N5f3
fRh7	R7h6

Red	Blue
K4h5	R6h5*c
K5h4	K6h5
K4b1	R5h6
S5f4	R6h5
S4b5	R5h6
	(draw)

	Red	Blue
c.	K5h6	K6h5
	K6b1	C6f6
	K6b1	C6h7
	R7h3	C7h8
	R3b5	C8f1
	R3b1	C8b1
	R3f8	K5f1
	P4h5	S4f5
		(draw)

	Red	Blue
d.	rRf4	R7h6
	K4h5	C6h5
	fRf1	R6f3
	K5f1	N3b5
		(draw)

	Red	Blue
e.	rRh8	N3f4*f
	R8f8	K6b1
	R5f1	R7f3
	K4f1	C6f2*g
	R5b3	R7b2
	K4b1	R7h5
	R5h6	K6h5
		(draw)

	Red	Blue
f.	R5b1	R7f3
	K4f1	N4b6
	K4h5	N6f7

Red	Blue
	(win)

	Red	Blue
g.	R5b2	R7b2
	K4b1	R7h5
	R8h6	R5b2
	R6f1	K6f1
	R6b5	
		(draw)

	Red	Blue
h.	R5h1	N4f6
	R1h4	K6h5
	R4f1	N6f4
	K4f1	R7f2
		(win)

	Red	Blue
i.	R5b3	R7b2*j
	K4b1	R7h5
	R5h6	K6h5
	S4f5	R5h6
	S5f4	R6h3
	R6h4	R3b5
	R4f1	
		(draw)

	Red	Blue
j.	R5h6	R7h6
	K4h5	R6h5
	K5h4	K6h5
	R6f5	K5h4
	R7b7	
		(draw)

	Red	Blue
k.	R5h4	K6h5
	R7h6	R7b1
	K4b1	R7b5*1
	R4f2	K5h6

	Red	Blue
	R6f1	K6f1
	R6b5	
	(draw)	
l.	R4b1	N4f6
	R4b1	N6f8
		(win)
m.	R7h6	N4b6
	R5h4	R7b1
	K4b1	N6f5
	K4h5	N5b4
	R4h6	N4b3
	R6h7	R7h4
		(will win)
n.	R7h1	N4f6*o
	R1h4	R7b4
	R4b1	R7h9*p
	R5b4	R9f3
	K4b1	R9b1
	K4f1	R9h8
	S4f5	R8f1
	K4b1	R8b1
	K4f1	R8f1
	K4b1	R8b2
	R4f4	K6f1
	R5h4	K6h5
	(draw)	

	Red	Blue
o.	R5h4	K6h5
	R1f4	K5f1
	R4f1	K5h6
	R1b6	
	(draw)	
p.	R5h4	R9f3
	K4b1	N6f4
	K4h5	N4f3
	K5h4	R9f1
	K4f1	K6h5
	S4f5	N3b5
	fRf1	N5f7
		(win)
q.	R5h6	R7h6
	K4h5	R6h5
	K5h4	K6h5
	R6f5	K5h4*r
	R7b4	
	(draw)	
r.	R7f4	K4f1
	R7h4	C6f8
	R4h3	K4h5
		(win)

· APPENDIXES ·

1 · The Secret Inside the Orange

This section contains the first two parts of *The Secret Inside the Orange* (1632) by Jin-zhen Zhu. A total of twenty complete games with variations is presented, categorized under six types of opening move. (The division between the two parts of the original is not shown.)

Lee Cannon-Vertical Rook (9 games)

	Red	Blue		Red	Blue
1.	C2h5	C8h5		C5f4*k	S4f5
	N2f3	N8f7		R9h6*l	R2f4
	R1f1	R9h8		R6f7	R2h5
	R1h6	R8f6		C3h1*m	R5b1
	R6f7	N2f1		C1f2	R8b2
	R9f1	C2f7		R3h5	
	C8f5*a,b,n,o	N7b8			
	C5f4	S6f5	c.	C5f4	N7f5
	R9h6	K5h6		C8h2	N5f6*d
	R6f1*t	S5b4		M3f5*g	N6f7
	R6h4	C5h6		R9h4*i	R1h2
	R4f6	K6f5		R4f1	N7f9
	C8h5			C2f2	S4f5
				R4f6	C5f5
a.		C2b2		K5f1	N9f7
	C8h3	C2h7		K5h4	
	C5f4	S6f5			
	R9h6	K5h6	d.	S4f5	N6f7
	R6f1	S5b4		C2b3*e	R1h2
	R6h4	C5h6		C2h5	S6f5
	R4f6	K6h5		R9h6	K5h6
	R4f1			C5f4	S4f5
				R6h5	
b.		R8b4*c			
	R6h3	R1h2	e.		N7b5
	C8h3	M7f9			

Red	Blue		Red	Blue
C2h5	S6f5	**i.**		N7b5
R6b5*f	K5h6		C2f2	S4f5
R9f1	K6f1		R4f7	N5b6
R9h4	S5f6		S4f5	N6b7
R6f5	C5b1		R6h5*j	N7b5
K5h4			R4f1	
f.		N5f7	**j.**		K5h4
R9h6	K5h6		R5h6	K4h5
R6h4	C5h6		R4h3	R1h2
R6f5	R1h2		R3b1	R2f2
R6h3	M3f5		R3h4	
R3f1	C2b7			
R4b1	N7b9			
R4h2	P9f1	**k.**		S6f5
R2f6	C2b1		C3h1	R8b2
R2h4	K6f1		R9h2	R8h6
C5h4			R3h2	R2f4
			C1f2	R6h9
			R2f1	R9h8
g.		N6f5	R2f8	
S4f5*h	R1h2			
R6h4	R2f4			
C2b3	N5f7	**l.**		P3f1
K5h4	S4f5		R6f7	N1f3
R9h6	C5h6		C3h1	N3b4
C2h5	R2h5		C1f2	R8b2
R4b1	R5f1		R3h5	K5h4
R4f2	S5b6		R5f1	
P5f1				
			m.		R8b2
h.		N5f7	R3b1	R5b1
K5h4	C5h6		C1h5	S5b4
R6h8	R1h2		C5h8	R8f7
R8f1	N1b2		C8b6	R5h6
R9h8			R3f2	S4f5
			C8h5	R6b2

Red	Blue
R3b2	R8h7
R3h7	

n.

Red	Blue
	R8h7
C8h3	R7h6
R6h3	M7f9
C5f4	S6f5
R9h2	R6b6
C3h2	C2b6
C5b2	C5f1
C2f2	R6f2
C2h1	M3f5
R3f1	R6b2
R2f7	M5b7
R2h4	

o.

Red	Blue
	S6f5
R9h4*p	R8b4
R4f7	R1h2
C8h3	R8h7
C5f4	R2f4
S4f5	R2h5
R4b2	M7f9
K5h4	R7b2
R6b4	C2b6
C5h8	R5h2

p.

Red	Blue
	R1h2
C8h3	C2b6
R4f7	R8b4
R4h3	M7f9
P3f1	R1f1
N3f4	C5f4
C5f4	C2h5
N4f5	R2f8

Red	Blue
C3h1*q	R8f6
R3f1	S5b6
R3h4	K5h6
R6f1	

q.

Red	Blue
	R8b2
N5f3*r	N1f2
N3f5*s	N2f3
C1h5	K5h6
R6f1	

r.

Red	Blue
	S5b6
R3h4	R8h9
N3f1	R9h8
C1h5	

s.

Red	Blue
	C5b4
R3f1	R8h7
N5f3	R2h8
C1f2	R8b8
N3b4	

t.

Red	Blue
	K6f1*u
R6b1*v	C5h6
C8h5	K6b1
C5h4	C6h9
R6h5	M3f5
R6h4	C2b7
C4f1	M5f3
C4h9	

u.

Red	Blue
R6f7	C5h7
fRh5	C7b1
C8f1	K6f1
R6h5	C7h6

	Red	Blue
	C8b1	
v.		C5h7
	R6h4	C7h6
	C8h5	R8b4
	R6h5	K6b1
	C5h4	C6f6
	C5h4	
2.	C2h5	C8h5
	N2f3	N8f7
	R1f1	R9h8
	R1h6	N2f1*[a]
	R6f7	P1f1
	P9f1	P1f1
	R9f4	C2f7
	C8f5	R8f2
	R6h3	R1h2
	C8h3	M7f9
	C5f4	S4f5
	R9h6	R2f4
	R6f4	R2h5
	C3h1	R8b2
	R3b1	R5b1
	C1h5	S5b4
	P3f1	N1f2
	N3f4	R5f3
	M3f5	N2f3
	C5b1	R5b3
	N4f5	N3f5
	N5f7	S6f5
	K5f1	
a.	R6f6*[b]	C2f2
	R6b2*[d]	P1f1*[f]

	Red	Blue
	N8f7	C2h3
	C8f5	C3f3
	C8h3	C7h3
	C5f4	S6f5
	R9f2*[i]	C7h8
	R9h6	K5h6
	R6f4	S5b4
	R6h4	C5h6
	R4f5	K6h5
	R4f1	C8b4
	C5b1	P7f1
	C5f1	
b.		C2f4
	N8f7*[c]	C2b2
	R6b2	C2h3
	C8f5	C3f3
	C8h3	C3h7
	C5f4	S6f5
	R9f2	R8f2
	R9h4	M7f9
	S4f5	R8h7
	K5h4	R7b2
	R4h6	
c.		R8f6
	R6h8	R8h7
	C5b1	C2h5
	N7f5	C5f4
	N3f5	R7h5
	C8h5	
d.		C2b2
	N8f7	C2h3
	R6f2	C3f4

Red	Blue		Red	Blue
R6b4	C3b2		C5f4	S6f5
C8f5	C3h7		R6h4	
R9f1*e	C7f3			
C8h3	C7h3	**g.**		N7b9
C5h4	S6f5		C5f4	S6f5
R9h6	K5h6		R9h6	K5h6
R6f6	K6f1		R6f4	K6f1
R6b1	C5h6		R6b1	C5h4
R6f6	C3b3		R6h4	C4h6
R6h5	C3h5		C8h5	C2b7
S4f5	C5b2		R6h5	K6b1
C5h4			C5h4	C6f3
			C5h4	
e.	R1h2			
C8h3	C7b2	**h.**		C5b1
R9h6	S6f5		R9h6	C5h9
C5f4	K5h6		R6f4	K5f1
R6f6	S5b4		C8f1	C9h2
R6h4	C5h6		R6f4	K5f1
R4f6	K6h5		R6b1	K5b1
R4h3	R8f7		R6b1	K5b1
N7f6	R8h7		R6h3	S6f5
N6f4	R7h6		C5f4	M7f5
R3f2	K5f1		R6h8	R1h2
R3b1	K5b1		R8h5	K5h4
N4f5	S4f5		R3f1	
R3h5	K5h4			
R5f1	K4f1	**i.**		R8f2
R5h6			R9h4	M7f9*j
			R6h4	R8b2
f.	P9f1	P1f1	S4f5	
R9f4	C2f5			
C8f5*g,h	R8f2	**j.**	C3f2	R8b2
R9h4	R1h2		C3h6	
C8h3	R8h7			

	Red	Blue		Red	Blue
3.	C2h5	C8h5	**c.**		C4h3
	N2f3	N8f7		N8f7	R8h7
	R1f1	R9h8		N3b5	C5f4
	R1h6	R8f6		N5f6	C3h4
	R6f7	N2f1		C6f5	C5b1
	R9f1*a	R8h7		N6b4	R7h5
	R9h4*d,e	C2h3		N7b5	S5f4
	R6b1	C3f4		N4f5	R5b1
	R4f6	S4f5		R6b1	
	C5f4	R7f1			
	S6f5	N1b3	**d.**		C2f7
	C8f6			R4f6	R1h2
				C5f4	S4f5
a.		S6f5		C8h5	R7f1
	R9h4	C2h4		R4h3	R7h6
	R4f7	R1h2		R3f2	R6b6
	C8f6	P3f1*b		R3b2	R2f2
	C5h8	N1f3		C5h2	R6h8
	C8f7	N3b4		R6h5	S6f5
	C8h7	R8h7		R3f2	
	N3b1	C5f4			
	C8b2	C4f2	**e.**		S6f5*f
	K5f1	R7f2		C5h6*g	C2f7
	K5f1	R7h9		C6f7	S5b4
	C8h7	M3f1		R6h3	S4f5
	fCh8	S5f4		R3b1	K5h4
	R4h6	C4b3		R4f7	R1f1
	C7f2	S4f5		R3f2	K4f1
	C8f1			R4h5	K4h5
				R3b1	K5b1
b.	C8h5	S4f5		C8f7	
	C5h6*c	C4f7			
	K5h6	R2f9	**f.**	R4f7	C2f7
	C6h5	C5h4		C8f5	N7b6
	C5f4			C5f4	R7f1

	Red	Blue			Red	Blue
	K5f1	C2b2			C8f6	C3b1
	K5h6	C2h4			R9h8	P3f1
	R6b6	R7h4			S6f5	P3h2
	K6f1	R1h2			C8h9	C3f6
	K6h5	R2f2			N9f7	R2f2
	K5h4				C9f1	N1b2
					C5h6	C3h7
g.		C2h4			R6f1	S5b4
	R4f7	R1h2			C9h7	S4f5
	C8f6	R7f1			C6f7	
	M3f5	C5f4				
	S6f5	R7b1		**b.**		C2h3
	C8h5	S4f5			N7f5	M7f5
	R4h5	N7b5			C8f5	N7f6
	R6f1				C5f4	R7f1
					S6f5	R7b2
4.	C2h5	C8h5			C8h5	N6b5
	N2f3	N8f7			K5h6	
	R1f1	R9h8				
	R1h6	S4f5		**c.**		P7f1*d
	R6f7	N2f1			N7f8	R7h6
	P7f1	R8f6			R9f1	P7f1
	N8f7*a	R8h7			R9h2	R6b5
	N7f6	P7f1			S6f5	P7f1
	N6f7*b,c	C2h4*g			C8h3	M7f9
	N7f5	M7f5			R2f7	R6h8
	C8f5	N7f6			C5f4	N7f5
	C5f4	R7f1			C3f7	
	C5h3	R7h2				
	C8h5	N6b5		**d.**	R9f1	R7h8
	C3f3				R9h4	P7f1
					N7f8*e	P7f1
a.		C2h3			R4f7	R1f1
	N7f8	P3f1			R6f1	S5b4
	N8f9	R1h2			N8b6	R1h4

Red	Blue		Red	Blue
R4h6	S6f5		R6h8	P7h6
R6f1	K5h4		N6f5	N7f5
C5h6			C5f4	R7f1
			R9f2*e	R1f2
e.	R8b5		R8h5	S6f5
R4f5	P7f1		C8f7	
C8h3	R8b1*f			
R4h2	M7f9	**a.**		P1f1
R2f3	N7b8		N8f7	C2h4
C5f4			N7f8	R8f4
			S6f5	P3f1
f. R4f2	R1f1		P7f1	R8h3
R6f1	S5b4		M7f9	R3f2
N8b6	R1h4		N8f6	R3h2
R4h6	C5f4		N6f4	C5h6
C5h6			C5f4*b	C4h5
			R9h6	
g. N7f8	C4h2			
R9f1	P7f1	**b.**		M7f5
R9h2	P7h6		C8h5	N1f3
R6f1	S5b4		C5h6*c	N3b4
N8b6	K5f1		C5f5	K5h4
R2f7			C5h3	
5. C2h5	C8h5	**c.**		N3f4
N2f3	N8f7		C5f5	S5b4
R1f1	R9h8		C5b3	R2b2
R1h6	S4f5		N4f6	R1f2
R6f7	N2f1		R6f1	K5f1
P7f1*a	R8f6		R6h5	
N8f7	R8h7			
N7f6	P7f1	**d.**		R2h4
P9f1	P7f1		N6f5	N7f5
P9f1	P1f1		C5f4	C4h2
R9f5*d	C2h3		R9h6	C2b2

Red	Blue
S6f5	
e.	R7h2
R9f2	R2h4
R9h7	R4b7
R8f1	R4h3
R8h7	
6. C2h5	C8h5
N2f3	N8f7
R1f1	R9h8
R1h6	S6f5
R6f7	N2f1
P9f1	R8f6
N8f9	R8h7
R9f1*a,b	C2h4
N9f8*f	R7b1
N8f6*h	R1h2
N6f4	R7f1
N4f3	K5h6
R9h4	C5h6
C8f6	C6b1
R6h5	S4f5
R4f7	K6h5
R4b3	K5h4
C5h6	C4h5
R4h6	
a.	R7h6
R9h2	P7f1
R2f3	R6h7
R2h4	P7f1
R4f4	R7h8
S4f5	P7f1
N9f8	C2f5

Red	Blue
N8f6	C2h7
N6f5	P7h6
C5h8	R1h2
C8f5	R2f2
N5f7	
b.	C2f2
R9h4	C2h7
N9f8	C7f3
C8h3*c	R7f1
R4f7	C5f4
S6f5*e	C5h7
S5f4	C7f3
S4f5	R7b2
C5f6	S4f5
K5h6	R7h2
R4h5	N7b5
R6f1	
c.	C5f4
S6f5	R1h2
N8f6	C5b2
N6f7*d	R2f2
R4f6	M7f5
K5h6	R7h5
C5f3	P5f1
R4h5	K5h6
R5h3	R5h3
R3f2	K6f1
N7f6	K6f1
R3b2	
d.	R2f9
K5h6	R7h3
R4f6	R3f2

Red	Blue
C5f4	S5f4
K4h5	K5h6
R6h4	K6f1
N7f6	K6b1
R5h4	K6h5
N6b5	S4f5
N5f7	

e.

Red	Blue
	R1h2
N8f6	C5b2
N6f5	R2f9
K5h6	R2h3
K6f1	R3b1
K6b1	C5h7
R6f1	S5b4
N5f7	

f.

Red	Blue
	R7b2
R9h4	P1f1
P9f1	R7h1
R4f7	P7f1
N3f2	P7f1
N2f3	C5f4
S4f5	R1h7
N8f6	R7h4
C8f5*g	N7b8
N3f2	R1h2
R4f1	S5b6
N2b4	

g.

Red	Blue
	N7b9
R4h1	R4h7
R1h3	R1h2
R3h1	S5b6
R3h4	K5h6

Red	Blue
R6f1	

h.

Red	Blue
	R7h4
N6f5	M7f5
C8f5	N7b6
R9h2	R1h2
C8h5	N6f5
R2f8	S5b6
C5f4	S4f5
R6h5	

7.

Red	Blue
C2h5	C8h5
N2f3	N8f7
R1f1	C2h4
R1h6*a	S6f5
P9f1*e	N2f3
N8f9	R1h2*g
R9h8*h	R2f4
R6f3	P7f1
N9f8	R2h6
N8f7*j,k	R9h8
C8h7	

a.

Red	Blue
	S4f5*b
C8f4	N2f3
C8h5	N7f5
C5f4	C4f7
R6f6	C4h2
R9h8	R1f2
K5h6	R9h8
R8f9	N3b2
R6f2	

b.

Red	Blue
P9f1	N2f1
N8f9	R1h2

Red	Blue
C8f2	R9h8
R9h8	R2f4*c
R6f3	R8f6
C5h8	R2h6
C8f4	R8h7
C8h9*d	R7f1
R6f3	S5f4
C8f7	K5f1
R8f8	

c.

Red	Blue
C5h8	R2h6
C8f4	R6h2
C8h9	R8f6
R6f3	R8h7
C8h6	R2f5
N9b8	C4f5
R6b2	C5h3
C9f1	M3f5
S6f5	N1b3
C9h8	P7f1
R6f6	C3f4
N8f9	C3b2
N9f8	R7f1
M3f5	R7b1
K5h6	S5f6
N8f6	P5f1
N6f7	C3b2
R6f1	K5f1
C8b1	N3b5
R6b1	

d.

Red	Blue
	C4b2
M3f5	P7f1
C8h6	C4f7
C9f1	N1b2

Red	Blue
R8f9	S5b4
R6f5	K5h4
R8b1	

e.

Red	Blue
	N2f1
N8f9	R1h2
C8f2*f	R9h8
R9h8	P7f1
C8h7	R2h1
R8f8	P3f1
R8h9	R1h2
R6h8	

f.

Red	Blue
	R2f4
C5h8	R2h6
fCh7	R6h3
N9f8	K5h6
R6h4	C5h6
N8f9	R3h2
C7f5	K6f1
R9h8	R9h8
C8h4	R2h6
R8f5	R6f2
C4f5	R6f2
C4h9	R8f7
S6f5	R8h7
R8h2	

g.

Red	Blue
C8f2	R2f4
R6f5	R9h8
C5h8	R2h6
R6h7	R8f4
fCh7	R6h3
R7b1	R8h3
C8h7	

	Red	Blue			Red	Blue
h.		R2f6	8.		C2h5	C8h5
	R6f3	P7f1			N2f3	N8f7
	R6h8*i	R2h3			R1f1	C2h4
	C8f1	R3b2			R1h6	S4f5
	S4f5	R9h8			C5b1	N2f3
	C8h7	R8f8			C8h5	R1h2
	C5h7				N8f7	R2f6
					P5f1	R2h3
i.		R2b1			N7f5	R9h8
	N9f8	P3f1			P5f1*a	P5f1
	C5h7	M3f1			C5f3*c	C4b2
	P7f1	P3f1			R6f6*d	N7f5
	N8f7	C4f1			C5f2	S5f4
	N7f9	C5h1			C5f5	
	C7f5	K5h6				
	C8f6	S5f6		a.		C5f2
	C8f1	S4f5			C5f3	P5f1*b
	C8h9	R9h8			N5f4	M3f5
	R8f9	K6f1			N4f5	M7f5
	C7f1	C4b2			C5f6	K5h4
	C9b1	N7b6			C5h7	R3h6
	R8h5				C7h3	P5f1
					R9h8	P5f1
j.		R6h3			R8f9	K4f1
	P7f1	R3b1			C3f1	R6b5
	C8h7				R8b1	K4b1
					R6f6	S5f4
k.		R6h2			R8f1	
	C5h7*l	R2b2				
	C8f2	R9h8		b.	R6f6	S5f4
	C7h8				N5f6	
l.		C5h6		c.		K5h4
	N7b8	R2h6			R6f5	C5f4
	N8f9				N3f5	R3h5

Red	Blue
M7f5	R5h7
rCh6	K4f1
R9h8	

d.

Red	Blue
	N3b1
N5f4	R8f2
N4f5	M3f5
R6h5	C6f6
R5h6	M7f5
C5f6	

9.

Red	Blue
C2h5	C8h5
N2f3	N8f7
R1f1	R9h8
R1h6*a	N2f3
R6f5*h,j	P5f1
R6h7	N3f5
C8f4	N5f7
P3f1	

a.

Red	Blue
	R8f4
N8f7*b	N2f3
R6f5	C5h6
P5f1*e	M3f5
N7f5	S4f5
P5f1	C6f1
R6f2	P5f1
R6h8	R1f2
N5f6*g	C6b2
N6f5	C6h2
N5f7	K5h4
C8h6	K4f1
C6b1	S5f6
R9f2	M7f5
R9h6	K4h5

Red	Blue
N3f5	P5f1
C5f2	R8h5
R6h2	

b.

Red	Blue
	R8h3
P7f1	R3f1
N7f6	P7f1*c
M7f9*d	R3f1
C8f7	R1h2
N6f8	R3b2
N8f7	

c.

Red	Blue
N6f5	N7f6
C8f7	R1h2
N5f7	

d.

Red	Blue
	R3h2
C8h7	N2f1
N6f7	R2b2
N7f8	S4f5
C7f5	R1f1
R6f7	N7f6
R9h7	N6f5
C7h9	R1b1
R6f1	S5b4
N8b6	K5f1
R7f8	

e.

Red	Blue
	C6f5
P5f1	C6h3
N3f5	C3f1
R9f1	C3h9
R6h7	N3b5
P5f1*f	C2f4
N5f7	R1f1

Red	Blue		Red	Blue
P5h4	M7f5		R6f3	K6f1
N7f6			C6f6	K6f1
			R6h4	
f.	C8f1			
R9h4	C8h9	**i.**	R9h6	R1h2
R4f7	R8f5		C8h7	P7f1
N5f4	N7f5		R6f7	C3h1
R7h5	C9h7		R7f3	R2h3
S4f5			C7f7	
g.	N3b4	**j.**		M3f1
R8f1	C6h5		R6h7	R1h3
C5f4	N7f5		C8h7	N3b5
C8h5	N5b7		R7h6	C2h3
N6f5	M7f5		R6f2	C3f5
C5f5	S5f4		N8f7	R3f6
C5h8			R9f2	R8f6
			N7b9	R8h7
h.	R8f6		R9h6	R3b6
R6h7	N3b5		S6f5	C5h2
N8f9	R8h7		K5h6	C2b2
R9f1	C2h3*i		R6f5	R7f1
R9h4	R1h2		R6h4	R7b3
C8h6	R2f4		C5f4	M7f5
S6f5	P7f1		R4h3	R7h5
R7h6	C3f7		R3h5	R5b1
C5f4	N7f5		R5b1	
R4f8	K5h6			

Lee Cannon-Horizontal Rook (2 games)

	Red	Blue		Red	Blue
1.	C2h5	C8h5		R2f6	R9h4
	N2f3	N8f7		R2h3	R4f6
	R1h2	R9f1		C8f2*a,c	R4b2

Red	Blue
C8h9	N2f1
P7f1	R4h3
M7f9*h,i	R3h2
N8f7	R2h6
R9h8	C2h3
N7f8	R6f2
N8f6	C3h4
C9h3*l	N7b9
C5f4	S4f5*m
R8f8	R1h2
R8h6	R2f2*n
C3f5	N9b7
R3f3	R6b6
N6f5	C4f2
R3h4	K5h6
R6f1	

a.

Red	Blue
	R4h2
C8h3	C2f7*b
R3f1	N2f3
C3f5	S6f5
C3h1*d	K5h6
R3f2	K6f1
P3f1	R1h2
R9h8	R2f2
C5h4	R2f7
N3f4	R2h6
N4f3	C5h7
S4f5	R6b5
R3b1	K6b1
M7f5	P3f1
N3f1	K6h5
N1f2	S5b6
R2b3	S6f5
R3f1	S5b6

Red	Blue
R3h4	

b.

Red	Blue
R9h8	R2f2
R3f1*c	M7f9
C3h2	N2f3
C2f5	S6f5
P3f1	R2b4
N3f2	C5f4
S4f5	R2h6
N2f3	R6h7
R3f2	S5b6
N3f1	R7b5
N1f3	K5f1
C2b1	

c.

Red	Blue
	N2f3
C3f5	S6f5
C3h1	K5h6
P3f1	R2b4
R3f2	K6f1
C5h4	C5f4
N3f4	S5f6
N4f3	K6f5
R3b1	K5b1
C4h2	C5h8
N3f1	S6b5
N1f2	S5b6
N2b3	C8b6
R3h2	C8h7
R2h4	S4f5
C2f7	K5h4
C1h3	K4f1
R3f4	K4f1
R4h5	R1f1
R5b1	M3f5

Red	Blue		Red	Blue
C3b2	M5b7		C5f4	S4f5
C2b2			R3h5	K5h6
			C5h6	C4f7
d.	S5f6		R5h6	K4h5
R3f2	K5f1		C3f5	
R3b1	K5b1			
P3f1	R2b2	**g.**		M7f5
R9h8	R2f4		C5f4	S4f5
N3f4	C5f4		R3h5	N2b3
C5h2	C5h8		C9h3	K5h4
N4f6	R2b7		C5h6	C4f7
N6f4	R2f2		R5h6	K4h5
N4f2	R1f1		C3f5	
N2f3	C8b6			
R3h5	K5h6	**h.**		R3h6
C2h4	S6b5		N8f7	P1f1
N3b4			R9h8	C2h3
			N7f8	P1f1
e.	C5h4*f		N8f6	R6f2
N8f7	R4b2		N6f7	R6h7
P7f1	R4h3		R3f1	C5f4
C8h9	N2f1		C5f4	R7h5
R9h8	C2h3		S4f5	R5h2
N7f8	R3f4		K5h4	R2f2
R8f9	R3h2		R3h5	S6f5
N9f7	N1f2		R5f1	
R3f1*g	M3f5			
C5f4	S4f5	**i.**		R3f3
C9h3	M7f9		C9h3	R3h2
R3h1			S4f5	C2f7
			R9h8	R2f1
f. S4f5	R4h2		R3f1*j	S6f5
C8h3	C2f7		C5f4	K5h6
R9h8	R2f2		R3f2	K6f1
R3f1	M7f5		C5h4	S5f4

Red	Blue		Red	Blue
R3h5	R2b4		N4f6	K5h4
C4b3	R2h7		C5h6	C7h4
P3f1	R1h2		N6f8	K4h5
N3f4	C5h6		C3f5	
N4f3	C6h7			
P3f1	S4f5	**m.**	R8f7	K5h4
P3h4	S5f6		N6f5	M3f5
P4f1	R2f4		R3f2	N9f8
P4f1	K6f1		R8h6	S5f4
R5h4			R3h6	K4f1
			C3h6	S4b5
j.	M7f9		C5h6	
C5f4	S4f5			
R3h1	K5h4	**n.**	R3f3	N9b7
C3f5	K4f1		N6f5	R6b5
R1h5	R1h2		C3h6	C4f7
C5h2	R2f2		R6f1	K5h4
C2f2*k	S5f4		C5h6	K4h5
R5f2			N5f7	
k.	S5f6	**2.**	C2h5	C8h5
R5f2	R2f2		N2f3	N8f7
C3b1	K4f1		R1h2	R9f1*a
R5h7	N1b2		R2f6	R9h4
C3b1	S6b5		R2h3*b	R4f7
C2b1	K4b1		N8f7	R4h3
R7b1	K4b1		C8f2	N2f1*e
C3f2			N3b5	C2h3
			C8h3	N7b9
l.	R6b5		C5h2	R3h4
C5f4	S4f5		C2f6	S6f5
S6f5	R1h2		C3f5	K5h6
R8f9	N1b2		R3f2	
N6f4	C4f1			
C5b2	C4h7	**a.**	R2f4	R9h4

Red	Blue
N8f7	N2f3
P7f1	R1f1
C8f2	R4f5
S4f5	R4h3
R9f2	P3f1
C5h4	R3b1
P3f1	R1h6
M3f5	R3f1
C8h4	R6h4
C4b1	

b.
	Blue
	N2f1
N8f7	R4f5
P5f1	R4h3
N7f5	C2f4
R3f1	C2h5
N3f5	R3h5*c
C8b1	R5b1
C8h5	R5h4
rCf5	S4f5
S6f5	R1f1
fCh3	M7f9
R3h1	K5h4

Red	Blue
C3f3	K4f1
R1h5	

c.
Red	Blue
R3f2	R1h2
R9f2	C5f3
C5b1*d	R5h7
C8h5	R7b6
C5f3	S4f5
C5f4	K5h4
R9h6	

d.
Red	Blue
	C5f3
S4f5	M3f5
R3b2	N1b3
C8h2	S6f5
C2f7	K5h4
R9h4	

e.
Red	Blue
R9f2	C2h4
C8h3	C4f5
R3f1	C4h1
C5f4	

Central Cannon-Horizontal Rook (2 games)

1.
Red	Blue
C2h5	N8f7
N2f3*a	N2f1*b
R1h2*d	R9h8
R2f6	P7f1
P5f1	S6f5
N8f7	C8h9
R2h3	M7f5
P5f1	P5f1

Red	Blue
N7f5	C9b1
N5f4*f	C9h7
N4f3	

a.
Red	Blue
	M7f5
R1h2	R9h8
R2f6	P7f1
N8f7	N2f1

Red	Blue
R2h3	S6f5
P5f1	C2h4
R9h8	R1h2
P5f1	P5f1
N7f5	R2f4
N5f7	P5f1
C8f2	P3f1
N7f5	C4h3
P7f1	P3f1
C8h5	R2f5
N5f6	K5h6
R3h4	S5f6
rCh4	C3f7
K5f1	R2b1
K5f1	K6f1
R4f1	K6f1
C5h4	

b.

Red	Blue
N8f7	M7f5
P5f1	S6f5
P5f1	P5f1
N7f5	R9h6
R1h2	C8h9
N5f7	P5f1
N7f6	C2h4
C8f5	R1h2
R9h8	R6f7
N6b5	R6h7
N5f4	R7h6
N4f3	K5h6
S4f5	R6b3
R2f9	K6f1*c
C8f1	N1b3
C5h4	R6h4
R2b5	

c.

Red	Blue
C5h4	R6h4
R8f4	C9f4
R8h4	S5f6
R4f3	K6h5
R2h5	K5h4
R4f1	S4f5
R4h5	N7b5
C4f6	

d.

Red	Blue
	C8h9
P5f1	M7f5
P5f1	P5f1
N3f5	C2h4
C5f3	S6f5
C8h5	R1h2
N8f7	R2f4
R9f1	R9h6
R9h6	R2b2
R2f7*e	N7f5
R2h5	M3f5
C5f2	S5f6
C5f4	

e.

Red	Blue
	C9f4
N5f3	C9b1
N3f2	C9h5
N7f5	C5f2
C5b3	R6f6
R2h1	R6h5
R1f2	N7b6
N2f3	

f.

Red	Blue
	R8h7
N4f5	M3f5
C5f5*g	S5b6

Red	Blue		Red	Blue
C8h5	N1b2		R8h5	K5h6
P3h5	N2f3		R5f1	K6f1
C5b2	S4f5		R5h4	
R5f2	K5h4			
R5f1	K4f1	**a.**		C6h5
R9f1	N3b2		N8f7	C5f3
R9h6	C2h4		N3f5	P5f1
C5h6	C4f6		R2f5	C5f2
C5h6			C8h5	S4f5
			R9h8	R1h2
g.	K5h6		R2h5	M3f5
C8h4	K6f1		N5f6	C2h1
C5h4	K6f1		N6f7	R2f9
R3h4	K6h5		R5h6	R2b9
C4h5	K5h4		N7f8	
R4h6				
		b.	N3f5	S4f5
2.	C2h5	N2f3	C5f3	R1h4
N2f3	N8f9		C8h5	P3f1
R1h2	C8h6		N8f7	C2f4
P5f1*a	M3f5		R2f7	C2h5
P5f1	P5f1*b		R7f5	R4f5
R2f5	S4f5		R9h8	R9h8
R2h5	R1h4		R2h4	K5h4
N8f7*d	C6f5		S6f5	S5f6
C8h9	C6h3		rCh6	R4h5
N3f5*i	R4f6		R8f4*c	R5h2
R9h8	C2h1		N5f6	R2h4
R8f7	C1f4		N6f7	
N5f6	N3b4			
C9f4	C1f3	**c.**		R5b1
C9f3*k	M5b3		N5f6	K4h5
R5f3	K5f1		N6f7	M5b3
R8f1	K5b1		R8f5	M7f5
N6f5	S6f5		C6f6	

Red	Blue		Red	Blue
d.	R9h8*e		N5f4	
N7f5	P9f1			
C8h9*f	R8f4		**g.**	C2h1
N5f4	P3f1		N5f4	R8f4
R5h7	R4f4		R8f7	C1f4
R7h6	N3f4		N4f5*h	R8h5
N4f6	C2h4		N5f7	R4f1
R9h8	R8h5		R8f2	
R8h5	R8f9			
S5b4	C9f4		**h.**	M7f5
N9f8	C9f3		C5f5	S5f4
S6f5	R8b1		R5h2	N9f8
M5b3	N6f4		C9h5	
K5h6	N4b5			
			i.	C3f1
e.	C8h9	P9f1	R9h8	C2b2
R9h8	C2h1		R5f2	M7f5
R8f7	N3f5		C5f5*j	S5f4
R8f1	N5b3		C9h5	R4h3
N7f5	C1f4		N5f6	K5h4
N5f6	P3f1		N6f7	K4f1
N6f5	M7f5		R8f8	
R5f2	R4f3			
R5f1	K5h4		**j.**	S5f6
C5h6	R4f4		C9h5	R4f3
R5f1			N5f6	K5h4
			C5h6	
f.	P3f1			
R9h8*g	C2b2		**k.**	N4f2
R5f2	M7f5		R8f1	R4f3
C5f5	S5f4		K5f1	R9h8
C9h5	K5f1		R8f1	S5b4
C5h7	K5h6		R5f2	S6f5
C5h6	C6h3		R8b1	

Central Cannon-Vertical Rook (2 games)

	Red	Blue			Red	Blue
1.	C2h5	N2f3			R6h7	C2h3
	N2f3	N8f9			M7f9	C8h6
	R1f1	M3f5			C8f2	R8f5
	R1h6	S4f5*a			N7f5	P5f1
	R6f5	R1h4			M9f7	R8f1
	R6h7	C2b2			N3f5	R8h7
	N8f7	C2h3			fNf4	S5f6
	R7f1	C8h3			N5f6	S6b5
	C8f7	C3f5			R7f1	K5h4
	R9f2	C3h7			R7h9	
	C5f4	C7f1				
	R9h6			**c.**		P3f1
					N7f5	N3b4
a.	N8f7	R1h4			R6f6	R8f2
	R9f1	R4f8			R6h8	N4f3
	R9h6	P9f1			R8h7	K5h4
	P5f1*b	R9h8			R7h6	K4h5
	P5f1	P5f1			R6h9	K5h4
	N7f5	C8h6			R9f2	K4f1
	N5f7*c	R8f4			N5f7	
	N7f8	N3b4				
	C8f5	C6h2	**2.**		C2h5	M3f5
	C5h8	P5f1			N2f3	N2f4*a
	C8f5	N4f3			R1f1	N8f9
	C8f1				R1h4	R9h8
					R4f7	N4f6
b.		P3f1			C5f4	S4f5
	P5f1	P5f1			C8h4*b	N6f7
	N7f5	C2f2			C4f7	
	P7f1	R9h8				
	R6f5	P3f1	**a.**	R1h2	N8f9
	N5f7	P5f1			P5f1	R9h8

Red	Blue		Red	Blue
P5f1	P5f1		N6f7	K4h5
N3f5	N4f6		C6f1	
R2f4	C2h3			
N5f6	R1h3	**b.**		K5h4
N8f7	P9f1		R9f2*c	C8f1
R9h8	S4f5		R9h6	C2h4
N7f5	C3h4		R6f5	S5f4
C8f7	C4b2		R4h6	K4f1
N6f7	C4h2		C4h6	S4b5
R8f9	R3h2		C5h6	
N7f8	C8h7			
R2h8	R8f4	**c.**		C8f2
N8b6	K5h4		R9h6	C2h4
C5h6	K4f1		R4f1	N6b5
N5f6	S5f4		R6f5	S5f4
R8f4	K4b1		R4h5	K4f1
C6f5	P5f1		C5b1	

Adverse Cannon (4 games)

	Red	Blue		Red	Blue
1.	C2h5	C2h5		R8h5	R8h5
	N2f3	N8f9		R6f5	R5b1
	R1h2	R9h8*a		R6h5	K6f1
	N8f9*f	N2f3*h		R5h4	
	R9h8*m	R1h2			
	P9f1*p	P9f1	**a.**	R2f5	N2f3
	R2f4*v,x	R2f4		N8f7	R1h2
	N9f8	R2h6		R9h8	R2f6
	R2h6*c',d'	N9f8		C8h9	R2h3
	N8f6*o'	P3f1		R8f2	C8h7
	N6f7	C8h3		R2h4	R8f8
	C8f7	S6f5		S4f5	R8h7
	C5f4	K5h6		N3b1	R7h9
	R8f8	R8f1		C9f4*b,c,d	N3f1

Red	Blue
C5f4	S4f5
R8f7*e	N1b3
R8h7	N3b4
K5h4	

	Red	Blue
b.		R9f1
	C5f4	N3f5
	C9h5	S4f5
	M7f5	R3h4
	R8f7	K5h4
	R8h7	K4f1
	R4h8	R4b3
	C5b2	P9f1
	C5h6	R4h6
	R8h6	S5f4
	R6f2	K4h5
	R7b1	K5b1
	R6f1	C5f5
	S5b4	

	Red	Blue
c.		S6f5
	C9f3	C5h6
	R4h6	M7f5
	R6f3	C7b1
	R8f7	K5h6
	C9h7	K6f1
	C7b1	K6b1
	R6h5	N3b5
	R8h6	

	Red	Blue
d.		P3f1
	C9h7	R3h4
	C7f3	S4f5
	C7h9	K5h4
	R8f7	K4f1

Red	Blue
R8b1	K4b1
C5h6	C5h4
N7f8	P3f1
N8f7	R9f1
M7f5	C4f5
R8f1	K4f1
R4h8	C4h3
R8f3	K4f1
C9b2	N3b2
R8b1	N2f3
R8h7	K4b1
R7f1	

	Red	Blue
e.		K5h4
	R8h7	K4f1
	R7b1	K4b1
	R4h8	

	Red	Blue
f.		P9f1
	R2f4	N2f3
	P9f1	P1f1*g
	N9f8	P1f1
	R2h6	R8f1
	N8f6	R8h4
	N6f5	R4f4
	N5f7	R4b4
	N7f9	R4h1
	R9f4	

	Red	Blue
g.	P9f1	R1f4
	R9h8	N9f8
	R2h6	R1h6
	N9f8	N8f6

	Red	Blue
h.	R2f4	R1h2

Red	Blue		Red	Blue
R9h8	C8h7		R4f5	K5f1
R2h6	R8f8*i		C8f6	
C5h6	S6f5			
P9f1	R2f6	**l.**		R1f1
C6f1	R2h3		N6f7	R1h6
C8f7	R3f1		N3f4	S6f5
C8h9	R3h7		C5f4	K5h6
R8f9	N3b1		C8h4	C5h6
C6h7	K5h6		C5h4	
R8b1	C5f4			
R6f5		**m.**		P1f1
			R2f4	R1h2
i.	P9f1*j	R2f4	P9f1	P1f1
N9f8	R2h6		R2h9	R2f4
N8f6	C7f4		C8h7	R2h6
N6f7	C7f3		R8f8	C5h6
S4f5	S6f5		C7f4	M3f5
C5f4	K5h6		R8h6	R6f3
C8h4	C5h6		C5f4*n	N3f5
N3f2	R6b1		C7f3	S4f5
C5h9	P3f1		R9f5	N5b3
R8f6			C7b1	
j.	C7f4	**n.**		S6f5
N9f8	C7f3		R6h5*o	S4f5
S4f5	C7h9		R9f5	N3b4
K5h4	R2h1		C7f3	N4f3
N8f6*k,l	N3b1		C7b1	
C5f4	S6f5			
R6h4		**o.**		K5h6
			R5f1	K6f1
k.	R1f2		R9h6	C6h7
N6f8	R8b7		R6f4	S4f5
R6h4	P9f1		C5h6	C7f4
N8f7	R8h3		R6h5	N3b5

	Red	Blue		Red	Blue
	C6f2	K6f1		C7f5	C7h3
	R5h4			R7f3	R6b2
				C5h7	R8h7
p.		R2f4*q		C7f7	S4f5
	R2f4	C8h7		C7h9	R7b1
	R2h6	R8f8		R7f2	S5b4
	N9f8	R2h6		R8h5	K5f1
	N8f6*s	R8h7		R7b1	
	S6f5	S6f5			
	C5h6	R7f1	**s.**		C7f4
	M7f5	R7b1		N6f7	C7f3
	N6f7	C7h3		S4f5	S6f5
	C8f7	K5h6		C5f4	K5h6
	C6f7	K6f1		C8h4*t	R6h7
	R6f4	R7b1		R8f4	C7h9
	R6h5	K6h5		R6h4	K6h5
	R8f8	K5b1		R8h6	R8f1
	C6b2			C4b2	R8b5
				C4f1	R7h4
q.	C8h7	R2h6		R6f1	R8h4
	R8f8*r	P9f1		S5f4	
	C7f4	N9f8			
	C7f3	S4f5	**t.**		C5h6
	C7h9	K5h4		N3f4	R6h7
	C5h6	C8f7		N4f2*u	C6h5
	N9f8	R6f3		R6h4	K6h5
	N8f6	R6h4		K5h4	R8b4
	N6f7	K4h5		R8f2	C7h9
	R8f1	S5b4		C4h3	R7h6
	R8h6			R8h4	
r.		P3f1	**u.**		R7h6
	P7f1	P3f1		N2b3	C6f5
	R2f4	C8h7		S5f4	R8f1
	R2h7	R8f8		N3f4	C7h4

	Red	Blue		Red	Blue
	K5f1	C4h2		R6f5	K5h4
	N4f3	K6f1		R8b1	
	N7f6	S5b4			
	R6h4		**y.**	C5h6	C8h7
				R2h6*z	R8f8
v.		C8h7		C6f1	R2h3
	R2h6	R2f4		C8f7	R3b2
	N9f8	R2h6		C6f6	S6f5
	N8f6	R8f8		C6b1	N3b2
	N6f7	C7h3*w		R8f9	R8b4
	C5f4	S6f5		N9f8	R3h2
	C8f7	K5h6		R8h7	S5b4
	R8f8	R8h7		C6h9	
	S6f5	R7b1			
	R8h5	C5f4	**z.**		S6f5
	K5h6	C5b5		C6f1	R2h3
	R6f5	C5b1		C8f7	R3f1
	R6h5	R6f1		C8h9	R3h7
	R5h4	K6h5		R8f9	N3b1
	R4b4			C6h7	K5h6
				R8b1	C5f4
w.	C8f7	S6f5		R6h4	C7h6
	R8f8	K5h6		R4f3	S5f6
	R8h5	C5f4		C7f6	
	C5h4	R6h4			
	R6h4		**a'.**		C8h7
				C6f1	R2h3
x.		R2f6*y		C8f7	R3f1
	R2h6	N9f8		C6h7	R3h7
	C5h6*a',b'	C8h6		R6f5	N3b4
	C6f1	R2h3		C7f6	K5f1
	C8f7	R3b2		R8f8	
	C8h9	S6f5			
	R8f9	N3b1	**b'.**		S6f5
	C6f6	S5b4		C6f1	R2h3

Red	Blue		Red	Blue
C8f7	R3f1		C5f4	R8f8
C8h9	R3h7		R8f8	R8h7
R8f9	K5h6		R6f5	N3b4
C9h7	K6f1		N7f5	S6f5
C7b1	K6b1		R8h5	K5h6
C6f6	N8f7		R5f1	K6f1
C6b1	S5b4		R5h4	
R8h6	C5b2			
R6h4			**f'.**	N8f6
			C5f4	S6f5
c'.	R8f1		R8f8*g'	N3f5
R8f1	N9f8		R8h5	K5f1
N8f6	R8h4		R6f4	K5b1
R8h6	R4f2		R6f1	K5f1
R6f8	R4f2		R6b1	
N8f7	R4b4			
R6f7	S6f5		**g'.**	N6f7
R6b3	K5h6		R8h5	K5h6
R6h4	C5h6		R5f1	K6f1
C5h4	K6f1		R6f4*h'	N3b5
R4f2	K6f1		R5h4	K6b1
C4b1			R6f1	K6f1
			R6h4	
d'.	P3f1			
N8f7*e'	N9f8		**h'.**	C5b1
C8f7*f',1'	N3b2		S6f5*i'	N3f5
C5f4	S6f5		N7f5	C8h6
R6f5	K5h4		C8b1	C6f1
R8f9	C5h3		N5b3	K6f1
R8h7	K4f1		R6b1	M3f5
R7b2	M7f5		C8b1	R8f4
R7h8			R5h4	C6b3
			R6h5	
e'.	C8f7			
C8f7	C5f4		**i'.**	N3b2

Red	Blue
N7f5*[j']	R6b2
R6h5	S4f5
R5b1	K6b1
R5f1	K6f1
R5h4	
j'.	N2f3
C5f2	R6b2
N5b6*[k']	N3f4
C5b2	S4f5
R6h5	
k'.	S4f5
N6f7	R6h5
N7f6	K6f1
R5h4	S5b6
R6h4	
l'.	S6f5
C8h9	C5h6
R8f9	M7f5
N7f5*[m']	K5h6
C9h7	K6f1
C7b1	S5f4
N5f6	K6h5
C5h8	N3f2
C7h9	
m'.	N3b1
C5f4*[n']	K5h6
R6f5	K6f1
R6b1	N1f3
R6h5	N3b5
C9b1	N5f3
R8b1	N3b5

Red	Blue
R8h5	K6b1
R5f1	K6f1
N5f7	
n'.	C8h5
R6f5	K5h4
R8b1	
o'.	N8f7
N6f7	C8h3
C8f7	S6f7
C5h6	R8f8
C6f7	N7f9
C6b1	M3f1
C6h9	K5h6
R6f5	
2. C2h5	C2h5
N2f3	N8f7
R1h2	R9h8
R2f6	C8h9
R2h3	R8f2
C8f2	C9b1
C8h3	C9h7
R3h4	N7f8
R4f2	C7f5
R4h8	N8f6
R9f2	R8h7
M3f1	C7h8
N3f4	R7f3
C5f4	S4f5
N4f6	C8f3
M1b3	R7f4
N6f8*[a]	R7b6
S4f5	R7h5

Red	Blue
N8f7	K5h4
R9h6	C5h4
R8b1	K4f1
N7f9	N2f1
R8h7	R5h7
N9b8	R7f6
S5b4	R7b5
S4f5	C4f2
R7b1	K4f1
N8f7	N1b3
R7f2	K4h5
R7b1	C4b2
R7h6	S5f4
R6f5	

	Red	Blue
a.		C8h6
	M7f5	C6b1
	K5f1	R7h4
	N8f6*b	C6b6
	N8f7	K5h4
	R9h6	C5h4
	R6f5	S5f4
	C5h6	S4b5
	C6b6	C6h4
	N6f8	C4h5
	N8f6	C5h4
	N6f5	C4h5
	N5f6	

	Red	Blue
b.		C6b7
	R9h6*c	R4h8
	R6f4	R8b6
	R6h7	R8h5
	R7f3	S5b4
	N8f6	C6h4

Red	Blue
R8h6	S6f5
R6f1	

	Red	Blue
c.		R1f2
	R8f1	R1h3
	R6f4	R4h8
	R6h7	R3f1
	R8h7	R3b3
	N8f6	K5h4
	C5h6	

	Red	Blue
3.	C2h5	C2h5
	N2f3	N8f9
	R1h2	C8h7
	R2f8	N2f3
	P7f1	R1h2
	N8f7	R2f6
	R9h8	R2h3
	C8f7*a	N3b2
	R8f9	R3f1
	C5f4	S6f5
	R2h5	K5h6
	R8h7	R3h4
	R5f1	K6f1
	R5b2	S4f5
	R7b1	C7b1
	C5f2	

	Red	Blue
a.		R9h8
	R2h4	S6f5
	C8h9	R3f1
	R8f9*b	N3b1
	R8b1	S5b6
	C5f4	

	Red	Blue		Red	Blue
b.		M3f1		R8h7	S5b4
	R8b1	N3b2		R4h6	S6f5
	R8h5			C5f4	K5h6
				R6h5	R3h4
4.	C2h5	C2h5		R5f1	K6f1
	N2f3	N8f9		R5b2	R4h7
	R1h2	C8h6		R7b1	K6b1
	R2f8	N2f3		R5h4	K6h5
	R2h4*a	S6f5		R4f1	
	P7f1	R1h2			
	N8f7	R2f6	**b.**	C5f4	R3h4
	R9h8	R2h3		S4f5	R4b4
	C8f7*c	R3f1		C5h1	
	C8h9	P7f1			
	R8f9	S5b6	**c.**		N3b2
	C9h7	S4f5		R8f9	R3f1
	C7b1	S5b4		C5f4	R3h4
	R4h6			R8h7	R4b6
				S4f5	R9h8
a.		S4f5		R7b2*d	C6h3
	P7f1	R1h2		K5h4	
	N8f7	R2f6			
	R9h8	R2h3	**d.**		R4f2
	C8f7	N3b2		R7h5	R4h5
	R8f9	R3f1*b		R5b1	

Screening Knights (1 game)

Red	Blue	Red	Blue
N2f3	C8h5	R9h6	R8h7*d
N8f7	N8f7*a	C2f7	N7b8
P3f1	R9h8	R2f9	R7f1*f
R1h2	R8f6	C8f4	P7f1
M7f5	P3f1	C8h1	M7f9
S6f5	C2h3	R6f8	N2f1

Red	Blue		Red	Blue
R2b3	P5f1	**c.**		S5f6
R2h6	S6f5		C1h3	S6f5
C1h5	K5h6		C3h7	S5b6
C5f2	S4f5		C7h4	
R6h5				
		d.	C2f6	R7f1
a.	P7f1	R9h8		C2h3	R7b1
	R1h2	R8f6		C3b2	R7h6
	M7f5	R8h7		C3f3	S6f5
	N7f6*ᵇ	P7f1		C3h1*ᵉ	K5h6
	C2f4	C5f4		C8f6	C3b1
	S6f5	C5b1		R6f9	K6f1
	C2h3	R7h4		R2f8	K6f1
	C3f3	S6f5		C1b2	N7b6
	C3h1	R4b1		R6h4	S5b6
	C8f2	R4h3		R2b1	
	C8h5	R3h5			
	R2f9	N7b6	**e.**		N2f1
	R2b5			C8f6	R1h2
				R6f8	C3b1
b.		N2f1		C8h9	R6b2
	C2f7	N7b8		R2f9	S5b6
	R2f9	R7b2		R6h3	R2f7
	S6f5	R7h4		R2h4	K5h6
	R9h6	C2h4		R3f1	
	N3f4	R4b1			
	C8f4	P3f1	**f.**	R6f8*ᵍ	N2f1
	C8h5	S4f5		R2h3	R1h2
	C5h1	P7f1		C8f6	C3b1
	N4f5	R4f1		R6h4	S4f5
	P7f1	R4h5		R4h5	
	C1f3*ᶜ	K5h4			
	C1h3	K4f1	**g.**		S4f5
	N6f7	N2f3		C8f6	R7b1
	N7b5			C8h5	R7h6
				C5b2	C5h7
				R2b1	

196 · APPENDIX 1

2 · The Plum-Blossom Meter

In this section is presented the complete set of thirty-one games with variations from *The Plum-Blossom Meter* (late seventeenth c.) by Zai-yue Wang. The games are categorized by six types of opening move.

Lee Cannon-Horizontal Rook vs. Vertical Rook (5 games)

1.	Red	Blue		Red	Blue
	C2h5	C8h5		R3h1	C5h7
	N2f3	N8f7		P5f1	R2h6
	R1h2	R9f1		P5f1	P5f1
	R2f6	R9h4		C3h2	C7h8
	R2h3	R4f6		N3f5	P5f1
	C8f2	R4h2		N5f3	
	C8h9*a	N2f1			
	C9h3*g	C2f7	b.		C5h6
	R3f1	S6f5		R3f2*c	C6b2
	R3f2	S5b6		P5f1	R2h6
	C5f4	S4f5		P5f1	P5f1
	R3b4	K5h4		R3b4	P5f1
	R3h6	C5h4		C3h2	R6h8
	C3h6	K4f1		R3b1	
	R6h5				
			c.		S5b6
a.		M3f1		P5f1*d	R2f2
	C9h3	N2f4		N3f5*f	S4f5
	R9f2	R2f2		P5f1	P5f1
	R9h6	R1f1		R3h2	C6h7
	R6f5	S6f5		N5f4	
	R6h7	N4b2			
	R7h8	R2b7	d.		C6h5
	R3f1	N2f4		R3b3*e	N4f6
	S4f5*b	M7f9		R3h4	S4f5

Red	Blue		Red	Blue
C5f4	K5h4		S4f5	R2f1
C5h1	R2h4		K5h4	C8b2
C1f3	N6b7		R4b1	
M7f5				
		i.		C2f7
e.		C5f3		C5f4	S4f5
C3h2	R2h8		C3f1	R1b1
P3f1	C5b1		R9h6	R2b4
P3f1	S4f5		R6f6	R2h5
P3h4	C5f1		C3h2	
P4f1	P5f1			
R3b1		**2.**	C2h5	C8h5
			N2f3	N8f7
f.		C6h5		R1h2	R9f1
R3b2	C5f3		R2f6	R9h4
C5f2	R2h5		R2h3	R4f6
C3h2	R5f1		C8f2	R4b2
N5f3			P7f1	R4h3
			C8h9	N2f1
g.		R2f1		M7f9	R3f3
R9f2*h	R2f1		C9h3	R3h2
S4f5	R2h3		N8f6	R2h4
R3f1	C2h7		R9h8*a	R1h2
C5f4	S6f5		S4f5*b,c	N7b9
R9h4	C7h8		R3f2	N9f7
R4f5	R3b3		R8f7	R2f2
K5h4	C8b2		R3b1*f	S6f5
R4h3	M7f9		C5f4	K5h6
R3h1			R3f2	K6f1
			C5h4	S5f4
h.		R1f1		R3h5	R2f3
C3f3*i	C2h7		C4b3	
C5f4	S4f5			
R9h6	C7h6	**a.**		C2h4
R3h4	C6h8		R8f8	R1h2

Red	Blue
R8h6	R2f9
S4f5	S6f5
C5h7	N1b3
R6h7	M3f1
C3f3	C4f7
C3h9	C4h7
C7b2	C7h3
C9f2	R2b9
R3f3	S5b6
R7h4	

b.

Red	Blue
	C2h4
R8f9	N1b2
C3f3	C4h7
C5f4	S4f5
R3f1	N2f3
C5h3	S5f6
R3h4	N3f5
R4b1	N5f3
R4h7	M3f1
M9f7	R4b4
P3f1	R4h5
C3h9	C5f4
N3f5	R5f2
C9h8	R5b2
C8h1	

c.

Red	Blue
	P1f1
R8f4	R4b4
R8h4	N1f2
R4f4	R2f3
R3f1*[d]	C2h7
C5f4	C5f4
N3f5	R4h7
N5f4	R2f2

Red	Blue
C3h7	M3f1
C5b3	N3f4
C5f2	

d.

Red	Blue
	N3f5
R3f2*[e]	C2f7
M9b7	S4f5
M3f5	R2f8
C3f4	K5h4
M5f7	

e.

Red	Blue
	S4f5
M3f5	C2b1
R3h2	C5h7
R4b2	C2f8
M9b7	R2f7
N3b4	R4f4
R4h5	R2h3
C3h5	C7h5
R5h4	K5h4
C5f4	

f.

Red	Blue
	M7f9
R3h1*[g]	C5h7
C5f4*[h]	K5f1
R1f1	K5f1
R1h3	C7f4
C3h5	K5h4
R3b1	

g.

Red	Blue
	R4b5
C3f5	S6f5
C3b3	P5f1
R1f2	S5b6
C3f3	S6f5

Red	Blue
C3b2	N4f2

	Red	Blue		Red	Blue
h.		R4b4	**b.**		P3f1
	C3h5	R4h5		C8h3	P3f1
	P3f1	K5f1		R9h8	C2h3
	R1f1	K5f1		R8f8	C3f5
	C5h2	R5h8		R3f1	
	N3f4	K5h4			
	C5h6	K4h5	**c.**		R7b1
	C2f1	R8b2		C8h3	R7b1
	N4f3	K5h6		P7f1	C2h4
	N3b5			R9h8	N2f1
				P7h6	
3.	C2h5	C8h5			
	N2f3	N8f7	**d.**		R7h6
	R1h2	R9f1		M7f9	N2f1
	R2f6	R9h4		N6f5	N7f5
	R2h3	R4f6		C5f4	S6f5
	R8f2	R4b2		R9f1	R6b4
	P7f1	R4f3		R3f3	R6b4
	N8f7*a	R4h3		R3h4	K5h6
	N7f6	R4h3		R9b4	C5h6
	C8h9*e	R3b3		R4h2	
	N6f4	N2f1			
	N4f3	R3h6	**e.**		M3f1
	R3f1	C2h7		N6f4	R3h2
	C9f3	P1f1		N4f3	C2h7
	C5f4	R1f2		R3f1	P1f1
	M7f5	S4f5		C5f4	S4f5
				M3f5	P1f1
a.		R4h7		C5h3	S5f6
	P7f1*b,c	C2h3		C3f3	S6f5
	C8h3	P3f1		R3b1	M1b3
	N7f6*d	N2f1		C3h1	K5h4
	N6f4	N7b9		R3f3	K4f1

Red	Blue		Red	Blue
R3h7		**b.**		C4h3
			N7f9	M3f1
4.	C2h5	C8h5	C9h3	C5f4
	N2f3	N8f7	S4f5	M7f5
	R1h2	R9f1	R8f3	C5b2
	R2f6	R9h4	R8h5	R6b3
	R2h3	R4f6	C3f3	C3h7
	C8f2	R4b2	R3f1	M1b3
	P7f1	R4h3	R3b1	C5f3
	C8h9	N2f1	R5b1	P5f1
	M7f9	R3h2	N3f5	P5f1
	N8f7	R2h6	N5f3	P5h6
	R9h8*a,c	C2h3	N3f4	S6f5
	N7f8	R6f2	R5f3	
	N8f6	C3h4		
	C9h3	N7b9	**c.**		R1h2
	C5f4	S4f5	C9h7*d	C2h4
	R8f8*g	R1h2	R8f9	N1b2
	R8h6	R2f2	N7f8*e	P3f1
	R3f3	N9b7	P3f1	R6h4
	N6f5	R6b5	C7f5	S4f5
	C3h6	C4f7	N8f9	R4b2
	N5f7		N9f8	C4h2
			C5h8	R4f4
a.		C2h4	N8b6	S5f4
	N7f8	R6f2	C8f7	K5f1
	N8f7*b	R6h7	R3f1	K5h4
	R7f8	S6f5	N3f4	C5f4
	C5f4	R7h4	R3b2	M7f5
	S4f5	R4b4	R3h6	
	R8f6	R4f2		
	N8b6	R4b3	**d.**		P3f1
	R3f1	K5h6	C7f5	S4f5
	R3f2	K6f1	C7b2	N7b9
	C5f4		C7h9	C5h1

Red	Blue		Red	Blue
C5f4	M7f5		N2f3	N8f7
C5b2	R6f2		R1h2	R9f1
N7f6	R6h7		R2f6	R9h4
N6f7	R7h4		R2h3	R4f6
N7f9	R2h4		C8f2	R4b2
S4f5	R4b5		P7f1	R4h3
R8f2			C8h9	N2f1
			M7f9	R3h6
e.	S4f5		N8f7	P1f1
N8f7	N2f3		R9h8*a	C2h3
P5f1*f	R6h5		N7f8	P1f1
S4f5	N3b1		N8f6	R6f2
C5h8	N1f2		N6f7	C5f4
C8f2	N2f3		S4f5*f	R6h7
C8h5	C5f3		N5h4	R7f2
K5h4			K4f1*g	R7b2
			R3f1	R7h5
f.	R6f2		R8f8	S4f5
C7b2	R6b1		R8h5	C5b5
P5f1	R6h3		R3h4	
N7f5	M7f5			
C7f5	R3b4		**a.**	C2h4
P5f1	R3f4		C9f3	R1f2
P5h6	C4h2		P3f1	R6f2
N3b5			N3f2	R6h8
			N2f1	N7f9
g.	K5h4		R3h1	R8b3
N6f5	M3f5		C5f4	S4f5
R8h6	K4h5		R8f8*b,c	R8h5
R6b1	P1f1		R8h6	R1h2
C3f5	N9b7		M3f5	R2f5
R6h5	K5h4		N7f6	R5f2
C5f2			M9b7	R2h4
			N6f4	R5h6
5.	C2h5	C8h5	P3f1	R4b3

Red	Blue
R1f3	

<table>
<tbody>
<tr><td>b.</td><td></td><td>C4b2</td></tr>
</tbody>
</table>

b.

Red	Blue
	C4b2
R8h6	R1h2
M3f5	R2f5
N7f6	R2h4
S6f5	R4b1
R1h3	R8b4
C5b1	R4h5
N6f7	R5f1
R6f1	K5h4
N7f8	K4f1
R3h6	C5h4
C5h6*c	S5b4
N8b6	K4h5
N6b4	K5b1
R6f3	K5h4
N4f6	

c.

Red	Blue
	S5f6
N8b6	K4h5
N6f7*d	K5b1
R6f3	

d.

Red	Blue
	K5h6
C6h4	S6b5
R6h4	S5f6
R4h5	

e.

Red	Blue
	K5h4
M3f5	R8h3
M9f7	R1h2
R8h7	R2h3

Red	Blue
R7h8	C5h8
R1h2	M7f5
C5f2	S6f5
R8h5	rRh2
N7f6	R3h4
R2h4	C8h6
N6f4	R2f7
S4f5	C4f7
R4f1	C4b1
S5b6	C4h6
N4b6	

f.

Red	Blue
	M3f5
R8f3	C5b2
R3f1	R1h3
N7b5	R6h7
K5h4	R7f2
K4f1	R7b2
N5b3	S4f5
C5f5	M7f5
R3h5	

g.

Red	Blue
	R7b1
K4f1	N1b3
R3f1	R1f4
R3h4	S6f5
R4f1	R1h8
R8f8	R8f4
C5f4	S5f6
N7f5	M3f5
R4f1	K5h6
N5b3	K6f1
R8h7	

Lee Cannon-Vertical Rook vs. Horizontal Rook (5 games)

	Red	Blue		Red	Blue
1.	C2h5	C8h5	**b.**		P7f1
	N2f3	N8f7		N6f7*c	C2h4
	R1f1*a	R9f8		N7f5	M7f5
	R1h6	S4f5		C8f5	N7f6
	R6f7	N2f1		C5f4	R7f1
	P7f1	R8f6		C5h3	R7h2
	N8f7	R8h7		C8h5	
	N7f6*b	C2h4			
	N6f4*d	R7h6	**c.**		C5f4
	N4f5*f	M7f5		N3f5	R7h5
	C8h5	R6b4		C5b1	C2h3
	C5f4	R1h2		C8f5	R1h2
	R9h8	P7f1		N7f5	R5f2
	N3f4*j	N7f6		S6f5	M7f5
	N4f6	N6f4		C8h5	S5f6
	C8h5	R6h5		C5h9	M3f1
	N6f4			R6b1	C3b1
				R6h4	N7f8
a.		C2h4		R4h9	
	R1h6	S4f5			
	N8f9	N2f1	**d.**		R7b2
	R9h8	R1h2		N4f5	M7f5
	C8f4	P3f1		C8f5	R1h2
	P3f1	R9h8		C8h5	S5b4
	R6f4	R8f6		N3f2*e	R7h8
	R6h7	C5f4		R9f1	R8f1
	N3f5	R8h5		R9h4	R2f1
	C8h3	M7f5		R4f6	
	R8f9	N1b2			
	R7f3	N2f1	**e.**		P3f1
	R7h6			N2f1	N1f3

Red	Blue		Red	Blue
N1f3	N3b5		fRb1	R2f1
C5f4	S4f5		fRh7	R2b1
R6b1			R7h6	M3f1
			S6f5	
f.	R1h2			
N5f3	R6b5	**j.**		R2f2
C8f6	R6h7		R8f7	R6f3
N3f4*g,i	R7h6		R8h7	N7f5
N4f5	N7f5		R7f2	S5b4
C5f4	C4h5		R6f1	K5f1
S6f5	R6f2		R6h5	K5h4
C8b2	R2f3		R5b2	
C5h8	P3f1			
R9h8	C5h2	**2.**	C2h5	C8h5
C8h6	C2h4		N2f3	N8f7
R8f6			R1f1	R9h8
			R1h6	S4f5
g.	C4h5		R6f7	N2f1
S6f5*h	R7h6		P7f1	R8f4
N4f5	R6f2		N8f7	P3f1
N5f7	R2h1		P7f1	R8h3
C5f5	M7f5		N7f6*a	C2h4
C8b1			N6f5	N7f5
			C5f4	R3f3
h.	C5f4		R9f2	R1h2
K5h6	M7f5		C8f2*b	R3h1
N4f5	R2f1		C8h6*d	C4f7
R6h8	N7f5		C6h3	M7f9
C5f4			K5h6	
i.	P1f1	**a.**		C2h3
N4f5	N7f5		S6f5	R1h2
C5f4	C4h5		N6f5	N7f5
R9f2	N1f2		C5f4	R2f4
R9h6	N2b3		M7f9	R3h5

Red	Blue
C8h5	R5h4
R9h6	R4b3
R6f8	R2f5
S5b6	C3f6
K5f1	N1f3
R6b2	N3b2
P3f1	R2b1
K5b1	

b.

Red	Blue
	R3b2
R6b1	R2f3
M3f5*c	R3h2
R9h7	rRh3
R7f4	N1f3
R6h7	M3f1
R7b1	R2h4
R7h9	M1b3
P3f1	

c.

Red	Blue
	R2h5
R6h5	M7f5
M5f7	R5h2
C8b2	N1f3
P3f1	

d.

Red	Blue
	C4h2
C6h3	M7f9
M7f9	C2f7
S6f5*e	R2f3
C5b1	R2h5
C5f2	R5b1
C3h5	P7f1
R6h8	C2h1
K5h6	N1f3
R8f1	

Red	Blue
e.	N1f3
R6b2	N3f2
K5h6	N2f3
K6f1	M3f1
C3h2	C2h1
R6f2	

3.

Red	Blue
C2h5	C8h5
N2f3	N8f7
R1f1	R9h8
R1h6	S4f5
R6f7	N2f1
P7f1	R8f4
N8f7	C2h4
N7f8	P3f1
P7f1	R8h3
M7f9	P7f1
S6f5*a	R3f2
N8f6	R3h2
N6f4	C5h6
C5f4	M7f5
C8h5	N1f3
C5h6	N3b4
C5f5	K5h4
C5h3	

a.

Red	Blue
	P1f1
R9h7*b	R3f5
M9b7*l	P9f1
M3f1	M7f9
P3f1	P7f1
M1f3*m	M9b7
M3b1	M7f9
M1b3	M9b7
N3f4	C5f4

Red	Blue		Red	Blue
K5h6	M7f5		C5f4*f	S5f6
N4f5	C5h4		R6b1	N1f2
N8f6	N7f5		N6f8	R1h2
C5f5	S5f6		K5h6	R6b3
C8h2	C4h8		R6f2	K5f1
N6f8	C4h2		R6b1	K5b1
C2h5*n	C8b3		C8f1	R6h5
fCf1	C2b2		R6f1	K5f1
R6h7	C2f2		R6h5	K5h6
N8f6	K5h4		R5b3	
C5h6	N5f4			
C5b2	N1f2	**d.**		C4h5
C5h6	N2b4		R5b1	R6h2
C6f4			R5b1	R2f3
			M9b7	C5f5
			M3f5	R2b7
b.	R3h6		N6f4*e	R2h6
P5f1*c	C5f3		K5h6	M7f5
N3f5*h	P5f1		R5f3	
N5f7	N7f5			
N7f6*j	N5b4	**e.**		N8b9
N6b4	C4h2		N4f5	M7f5
R7f5	C2f5		N5f3	N9b7
R7h5*k	C5h8		R6h3	R2h4
N4f3	K5h4		R3h4	
N8f6	R1f1			
N3f4	S5b6	**f.**		S5b4
C5h6	C8h4		R6b1*g	R6b3
N6f7	R1h3		N6f7	K5f1
S5f4			K5h6	K5h6
			R6h4	R6b1
			N7f6	K6h5
c.	R6f2		C8h5	
N8f6	C5f3			
C8f5	N7f8	**g.**		N1f2
R7f6	P5f1			
R7h5*d	C5b2			

Red	Blue		Red	Blue
R6h2	R1f3		R5b1	M3f5
N6f5	S4f5		N4f6	R1h4
N5b7	M3f5		N6f4	S5f6
C5h9			R5f3	S6b5
			R5h9	
h.	C5f2			
M3f5	R6h5	**l.**		N7f6
N5f6	R5f3		C5f4	N6f4
N6f4	C4h6		N8f6	R1h2
N8b7	R5b3		N6f4	
N7f6*i	N1f2			
N6f7	R5h6	**m.**		N7f9
C8h5	N2b3		N3f4	C5h8
N7f5	M7f5		M3b1	N9f7
C5f5	S5b4		N4f5	
R7f7				
		n.		N1f2
i.	R1h2		rCf1*o	C8b3
C8f5	N7f6		R6b3*p	C8h2
N6f7	R5f2		R6f4	K5f1
N7f8	R2h1		R6b1	K5b1
R6f1	S5b4		C5h2	N5b7
N8b6	K5f1		C2h5	C2h5
R7f8			fCh3	
j.	R6f2	**o.**		N2f3
R6h8	R6h2		C5h3	N5f7
N8f7	R2b5		C5b2	N3f2
N7f8	C5f1		K6h5	C8h1
N8b6	S5f4		C3h5	N7f5
N6f8	R1f1		rCh2	
R7f9	K5f1			
R7b6		**p.**		M3f5
			N8f6	K5f1
k.	N4f3		R6h8	R1h2

Red	Blue		Red	Blue
N6b5		**b.**		R8f6
			C5h8	R2h1
4. C2h5	C8h5		R9f1	R8h7
N2f3	N8f7		M3f5	R7h6
R1f1	R9h8		R9h2*c	P7f1
R1h6	S6f5		R2f7	P7f1
R6f7	N2f1		P7f1	P7f1
P9f1*a	R8f6		fCb1	C5f4
N8f9	R8h7		N3f5	R6h5
R9f1*f	C2f2		C8f4*d,e	N7f6
R9h4	C2h7		R2f1	R5h2
N9f8	C7f3		R2h3	S5b6
C8h3	C5f4		C8h6	S4f5
S6f5	R7f1		C8f1	R2h4
N8f6	C5b2		C8h5	R4f1
R4f7	R1h2		C5h1	
N6f5	R7h5			
N5f3		**c.**		C5h6
			C8h5	C4h5
a.	C2h4		C5f3	M7f5
N8f9	R1h2		N9f8	P7f1
C8f2*b	R2f4		N3f2	P7f1
R9f1	R8f6		N2f3	R6b3
C5h8	R2h6		N8f6	R6h7
fCh7	R6h3		R2f7	R1h2
R9h4	C5h6		C8f6	
N9f8	K5h6			
N8f9	R3h2	**d.**		R5h2
C7f5	K6f1		C8h3	R2f1
C7b2	C4f2		R2h4	C4h6
C7h3	C4h6		C3h2	R1h2
R4f4	R2h6		C2f2	
C3h9	R6h2			
C9f1	K6b1	**e.**		C4f2
N9f8			C8f4	C4h5

<table>
<thead>
<tr><th>Red</th><th>Blue</th><th></th><th>Red</th><th>Blue</th></tr>
</thead>
<tbody>
<tr><td>S6f5</td><td>R5h6</td><td></td><td>C5h8</td><td>R2h1</td></tr>
<tr><td>R2h3</td><td>K5h6</td><td></td><td>M7f5</td><td>P7f1</td></tr>
<tr><td>K5h6</td><td></td><td></td><td>N9f8</td><td>N7f6</td></tr>
<tr><td></td><td></td><td></td><td>N8f6</td><td>C3b1</td></tr>
<tr><td>f.</td><td>C2h4</td><td></td><td>P9f1</td><td>P1f1</td></tr>
<tr><td>N9f8</td><td>R7b1</td><td></td><td>R9f5</td><td></td></tr>
<tr><td>N8f6</td><td>R7b1</td><td></td><td></td><td></td></tr>
<tr><td>N6f5</td><td>M7f5</td><td>b.</td><td></td><td>S6f5</td></tr>
<tr><td>C8f5</td><td>N7b6</td><td></td><td>N9f8*c</td><td>C3f5</td></tr>
<tr><td>R9h2</td><td>R1h2</td><td></td><td>N8f7</td><td>R7f1</td></tr>
<tr><td>C8h5</td><td>N6f5</td><td></td><td>N7f9*f</td><td>C5h1</td></tr>
<tr><td>R2f8</td><td>S5b6</td><td></td><td>R8h3</td><td>M7f5</td></tr>
<tr><td>C5f4</td><td>N5b7</td><td></td><td>R3f1</td><td>C1b1</td></tr>
<tr><td>R6h4</td><td></td><td></td><td>C5f4</td><td>R7h6</td></tr>
<tr><td></td><td></td><td></td><td>C8h5</td><td></td></tr>
<tr><td>5.</td><td>C2h5</td><td></td><td></td><td></td></tr>
<tr><td>N2f3</td><td>N8f7</td><td>c.</td><td></td><td>R7f1</td></tr>
<tr><td>R1f1</td><td>R9h8</td><td></td><td>N8f6*d</td><td>R7b3</td></tr>
<tr><td>R1h6</td><td>N2f1</td><td></td><td>N6f5</td><td>M7f5</td></tr>
<tr><td>R6f7</td><td>R8f6</td><td></td><td>R6h7</td><td>R2h1</td></tr>
<tr><td>P9f1</td><td>C2h3</td><td></td><td>R7h6</td><td>N7b6</td></tr>
<tr><td>N8f9</td><td>R1h2</td><td></td><td>C5f4</td><td>R7h5</td></tr>
<tr><td>C8f6*a</td><td>C3b1</td><td></td><td>C8h5</td><td></td></tr>
<tr><td>R9h8</td><td>R8h7</td><td></td><td></td><td></td></tr>
<tr><td>R8f7*b</td><td>R7f1</td><td>d.</td><td></td><td>C5h4</td></tr>
<tr><td>R6h7</td><td>C5f4</td><td></td><td>R6h7</td><td>R7b3</td></tr>
<tr><td>S6f5</td><td>M3f5</td><td></td><td>N6f4</td><td>C4h6</td></tr>
<tr><td>N9f8</td><td>C5h7</td><td></td><td>R7h6*e</td><td>C6b1</td></tr>
<tr><td>S5f4*g</td><td>R7h6</td><td></td><td>N4f3</td><td>K5h6</td></tr>
<tr><td>N8f6</td><td>R6b3</td><td></td><td>C8h5</td><td>S4f5</td></tr>
<tr><td>R7h6</td><td>C7b2</td><td></td><td>R8h4</td><td>R2f1</td></tr>
<tr><td>N6f7</td><td>R2h3</td><td></td><td>R6b4</td><td>R2f3</td></tr>
<tr><td>R8h9</td><td></td><td></td><td>C5h4</td><td></td></tr>
<tr><td></td><td></td><td></td><td></td><td></td></tr>
<tr><td>a.</td><td>R8h7</td><td>e.</td><td></td><td>R7h6</td></tr>
</tbody>
</table>

Red	Blue
C5f4	K5h6
C5h9	R6f5
K5f1	C6h5
M7f5	P7f1
N4b6	N7f6
C9h1	

	Red	Blue
f.		R2h1
	R8h5	M7f5
	N9f7	K5h6
	R6b4	R7h6
	S6f5	R6b1
	C5h4	R6f1

Red	Blue
S5f4	C3b4
C8b7	

	Red	Blue
g.		C7f3
	S4f5	R7b3
	N8f7	S6f5
	N7f9	C7h3
	R7h6	R2h3
	C5h7	R3f6
	R8b4	R3f1
	C8f1	R3b7
	R6f1	

Adverse Cannon (5 games)

	Red	Blue
1.	C2h5	C2h5
	N2f3	N8f9
	N8f9	N2f3
	R1h2	R9h8
	R2f4	R1h2
	R9h8	R2f4
	P9f1	R2h6
	N9f8	P3f1
	P7f1	C8h7
	R2h6*a	P3f1
	R6h7*e	N3f4
	R7f5*f	N4f6
	N8f6*g	N6f7
	R7h6	K5h4
	C8h6	K4h5
	R8f9	K5f1
	R8b1	K5b1
	C5f4	C5h4

	Red	Blue
	N6f5	S6f5
	R8h5	
a.		R8f8
	C5h7	P9f1
	C7f3	M3f1
	N8f7*b	S6f5
	C7f2	C7h3
	C8f7*d	M1b3
	R8f8	R8h7
	R8h7	R7b1
	R7f1	K5h6
	R7b2	K6f1
	C8b1	K6b1
	S6f5	C5f4
	K5h6	M7f5
	R7h5	C5b4
	N7f5	

	Red	Blue			Red	Blue
b.		N9f8			N3f4	R4f3
	C8f7*c	M1b3			S4f5	C7h5
	R6f5	N3b4			N4b6	R4b1
	C7f4				K5h4	
c.		N3b2		**g.**		R6h4
	R6f5	K5h4			C8f7	R8f4
	R8f9				R8f8*h	N6f5
					M3f5*i	C7f4
d.		C3b2			C8h9	C5h1
	R8f8	C5h3			R7b4	S4f5
	R6f4	R8b7			R8f1	S5b4
	R8h7	C3f3			R8b4	
	N7f9					
				h.		C7f4
e.		C5h6			C5h7	C7f3
	C8h7	M3f5			S4f5	N6f7
	N8f9	N3f1			R7h6	
	R8f6	C6f1				
	C5f4	S6f5		**i.**		C5h1
	R7h4	R6h3			P3f1	C1b2
	R4f2	R3f3			R7b1	S4f5
	R4f2	R3b7			N3f4	R4h6
	S4f5	R8f2			R7f1	S5b4
	R4b1				R7b2	S4f5
					R8h6	
f.		N4f2				
	R7b5	R8f8		**2.**	C2h5	C2h5
	R7h8	C7f4			N2f3	N8f9
	C5f4	S6f5			N8f9	N2f3
	R8h4	R6h2			R1h2	R9h8
	C8h7	R2h3			R2f4	R1h2
	R8f5	R8b4			R9h8	R2f4
	R4f4	R8h4			P9f1	R2h6
	R8f2	C7b2			N9f8	P3f1

Red	Blue
P7f1	P9f1
P7f1	N9f8
R2h6*a	N8f6
P7f1	N6f7
C8h3	C8f7
S6f5	C5f4
K5h6	S6f5
P7f1*c	M7f5
C5f4	K5h6
C3h4	R6h2
N8f6	R2f5
N6b4	C5h6
R6f5	S5b4
N4f3	C6h5
N3b4	C5h6
N4f2	C6h5
N2f3	K6f1
N3b4	C5h6
N4b5	

	Red	Blue
a.		R6h3
	C5h7*b	N8f7
	C7f2	M3f1
	N8f9	N3h2
	N9f7	C8h3
	C7h8	R2h3
	C8f5	S4f5
	C8f6	C3f7
	C6f5	S5f4
	rCh9	R3b3
	C9f1	K5f1
	R6h7	R3h1
	R8h7	
b.		R3f2

Red	Blue
C8b1	M3f1
C8h7	R3h1
N8f7	S6f5
C7f5	C8h3
C7f6	M1b3
R8f8	C5h6
R8f1	M7f5
C7h4	S5f6
N7f5	

	Red	Blue
c.		K5h6
	C3h4	R6h2
	C5f4	R8f4
	R8f3	C8b3
	R6h4	S5f6
	R4f3	K6h5
	R8h6	
3.	C2h5	C2h5
	N2f3	N8f9
	N8f9	N2f3
	R1h2	R9h8
	R2f4	R1h2
	R9h8	R2f4
	P9f1	C8h7
	R2h6	R8f8
	N9f8	R2h6
	N8f6*a	C7f4
	N6f7	C7f3
	S4f5	S6f5
	C5f4	K5h6
	C8h4	C5h6
	N3f2*j	R6b1
	C5h9	P3f1
	R8f6	

	Red	Blue
a.		S6f5
	N6f7	C7h3
	C8f7*b	R6f3
	S6f5*g	C5f4
	K5h6	K6h7
	C5f4	K5h6
	R8f7*h	C3h4
	R6h4	C4h6
	R4f3	S5f6
	R8h4	K6h5
	C8b2	R7h4
	S5f6	C5h4
	S6b5	K5f1
	R4h6	C4h9
	R6f1	K5f1
	C5h6	
b.		R8h7
	R8f2*c	K5h6
	C5h4*e	C5h6
	R8f6	R6f3
	R8h5	C6h4
	S6f5	R6b5
	R5h6	K6h5
	rRh8	
c.		R7f1
	S6f5*d	P9f1
	C5f4	K5h6
	M7f5	R7b2
	C5f2	
d.		C5h8
	R6h2	M7f5
	C5f4	P9f1

	Red	Blue
	R8h6	K5h6
	C5f2	C3h4
	R2f3	C4h8
	R6f7	K6f1
	C5h9	
e.		K6h5
	C4f2	R7f1
	S6f5	C5h8
	C4h5*f	R6h5
	R8h4	R7b1
	M7f5	C8f7
	M5b3	C8h9
	N3b1	R7h9
	R4f6	C3h4
	R6f2	R9h7
	C5h7	R5h3
	R6h5	
f.		C3h5
	C5h2	R7b1
	C8h9	C5h4
	R6f2	C8f1
	R6h7	M7f5
	R8f7	K5h6
	R8b1	
g.		R6h7
	C5f4	K5h6
	R6h4	C5h6
	R8f8	R8b7
	C8h6	
h.		R8b6
	R6h4	C3h6

Red	Blue		Red	Blue
C5h9	R8f2		N8f9	N2f3
M7f5	R8h4		R1h2	R9h8
K6h5	M7f5		R2f4	R1h2
C9f3	N9b7		R9h8	R2f6
R8f1*i	R4f4		S6f5	C8h7
C9h7	M5b3		R2h6	R8f8
R8h5	R4b6		P3f1	P7f1
R5b5	R7h8		C5h6*a	P7f1
R5f5	N7f9		C6f1*b	R2b2
R5h1	R8b5		P9f1*c,d	C7f5
R4h8	C6h7		N9f8	R2h6
R8f4	R4h6		N8f6	C5f4
R8h6	C7b2		K5h6*e	N3b2
R1h3	R8h7		C8h5	N2f1
R3f1	R7b2		C5f4*f	R6b2
R6f1	K6f1		R8f8	R8b5
R6b1			N6f5	S6f5
			R6f5	K5h4
			R8h6	

	Red	Blue			Red	Blue
i.		R7b1				
	R8h5	C5b5				
	R4f3	C5h6				
	R4h5	C6h3		**a.**		C7f3
	R5h4	K6h5			M7f5	C7f1
	R4f1	C3f5			R6f3	N3b1
	M5f7				R6f1	N1f3
					R6h7	N3b5
					R7h6	N5f7
j.		C6f5			C6f7	S6f5
	N2f4	C6h9			R6h7	S5b4
	C5h1	C9b4			R7f1	C5h6
	N7f5	S4f5			R8h6	C6b2
	R6h4	K6h5			C8h7	R2f1
	R8f9				C7f4	R2h1
					R6f8	R1f2
					S5b6	R8h6
4.	C2h5	C2h5			R7h9	
	N2f3	N8f9				

	Red	Blue
b.		R2h3
	C8b1	R3h4
	R6b1	R8b1
	M7f5	R8h7
	N9f7	P3f1
	N7f6	N3f4
	R6f2	C5f4
	C8h7	M7f5
	R8f6	P7h6
	K5h6	S6f5
	R8h5	C5h3
	R5b3	C3f1
	R6b3	C7f1
	C7h6	C7h3
	C6f8	rCb1
	C6b1	
c.		P7f1
	N9f8	R2h6
	N8f6	P7f1
	M3f5	P7f1
	N6f7	C7h3
	C8f7	S6f5
	C6f6	P7h6
	C6b1	S5b4
	C6h3	P6h5
	S4f5	
d.		R2h6
	N9f8	P3f1
	N8f9	N3f1
	C8f7	S6f5
	C6f6	
e.		N3b1

	Red	Blue
	C8f7	C5h7
	C6h5	S6f5
	N6f4	C7f3
	K6f1	C7f1
	K6f1	R8b1
	M7f5	N1f3
	R8f8	R6b1
	R8h5	K5h6
	R5f1	K6f1
	R6f4	N3b5
	R5h4	
f.		R8b6
	R8f8	R6h5
	N6f5	S6f5
	R6h3	K5h6
	R3h4	
5.	C2h5	C2h5
	N2f3	N8f9
	N8f9	N2f3
	R1h2	R9h8
	R2f4	R1h2
	R9h8	C8h7
	R2h6	R8f8
	C5h7*a	R2f6
	C7f4	M3f1
	P9f1	C7f4
	M3f5*e	S4f5
	N9f8*j	R2h3
	N8f9*o	R3b3
	N9f7*p	R3h2
	P9f1	R2f3
	P9f1*r	M1b3
	R6f4	R2b4

Red	Blue
R6h7	S5b4
C8h7	R2f7
R7h6	

a.

Red	Blue
	R8h3
C7f4	R3b2
C7b2	C3f1
C7h8*b	R2f5
R6h8	R3h7
M7f5	C5f4
S6f5	R7b1
C8h7*d	M3f5
N9f7	C5b2
C7f5	C7h3
N7f6	C3f2
rRf3	R7f3
K5h6	R7b2
N6f7	S6f5
R8f5	

b.

Red	Blue
	R2h1
M3f5	R3b3
fCh7	R3h4
R6f1	N3f4
C8f7*c	N4f6
C7b2	N6f7
N9f7	C5f4
S4f5	M7f5
N7f6	R1f1
C7h3	C5b2
R8f6	R1h8
C3b2	

c.

Red	Blue
	N4f5
C7b3	N5f7

Red	Blue
N9f7	C5h3
N7f6	C3h4
M5f7	

d.

Red	Blue
	N3f4
fRh7	M3f5
R7h6	R7h6
K5h6	N4b3
R8f6	S6f5
R8h7	N3b1
R6b1	P5f1
C7h6	M5b3
N9f7	

e.

Red	Blue
	S6f5
N9f8	R8h7
C7h8	R2h3
S4f5	P9f1
C8f3	N3b2
C8f7*f	R3b6
N8f7	R7b1
N7f9*h	C7h8
N9f7	K5h6
R6h4	C5h6
R8f7*i	C8b5
R8h4	S5f6
R4f3	C8h6
N7b5	K6h5
R4f1	

f.

Red	Blue
	M1b3
N8f6	R7b1
R6h4	R3b2
N6f5	M7f5
R8f7*g	N9f8

Red	Blue
R4f4	R3b3
R8h5	R3h2
K5h4	N8b7
M5f3	R2b1
R5h3	

g.

Red	Blue
	M5b7
R8f1	N9f8
R4f4	N8b7
R8h6	

h.

Red	Blue
	N9f8
R8f5	N8f9
R6f5	S5b4
N9f7	

i.

Red	Blue
	C6b1
R8h3	C8h7
M5f3	

j.

Red	Blue
	R8h7
C7h8	N3f2
R6h7	R7b1
rCh3	R2f3
C8f3*k,l	S5f4
R7f5	K5f1
R7b3*n	R2b3
N8f6	N2f4
C8h3	

k.

Red	Blue
	C5f4
S4f5	R2h3
R7f5	S5b4
R7b4	S4f5
R7h8	R3b3

Red	Blue
N8f6	R3h4
C8h9	

l.

Red	Blue
	K5h4
R7f5	K4f1
R7b3*m	C5f4
S4f5	R2h3
N8f6	C5b2
C8h3	C7b6
R7f2	K4f1
K5h4	R3h2
N6f8	K4h5
R7b2	C5h6
R7h5	K5h6
R5h4	K6h5
R4b1	

m.

Red	Blue
	K4b1
N8f6	N2f4
R7h6	C5h4
N6f8	N4f2
C3b1	

n.

Red	Blue
	K5b1
R7h5	N2f4
R5f1	M7f5
C8b9	N4f6
N8f6	N6f7
K5f1	C7h8
C3h2	M1b3
P7f1	P9f1
C8f1	N7b6
C2h4	N6b7
N6f8	

	Red	Blue			Red	Blue
o.		N3f1			R7f1	
	C8f7	R3b3				
	C8h9	C5h4		r.		R8h7
	R8f9	S5b4			N7b6*s	R7b1
	R6f3	M1b3			N6f8	C5h2
	C9h7	R3b3			R6f2	M1b3
	R8h7	S6f5			R8f1	M7f5
	R6b3				R8h7	R2f1
					R6f2	S5b4
p.		R3b1			N8f6	
	C8f7*q	S5f4				
	R8f8	R8h3		s.		M1f3
	C8h9	rRb1			P9h8*t	R7b1
	R8f1	K5f1			N6f5	M3b5
	R6h4				R8h9	S5b4
					R9f9	S6f5
q.		R3h4			C8h3	R2b3
	R6h7	R8h7			C3b1	
	C8h9	R7b1				
	R8f9	S5b4		t.		R2b3
	R8b1	S4f5			R8h9	R2b3
	R7f5	S5b4			N6f7	R2h3
	M5f3	R7f2			N7f9	R3h4
	R7b2	S4f5			R6f5	
	R8f1	R4b2				

Screening Knights vs. Central Cannon (8 games)

	Red	Blue		Red	Blue
1.	C8h5	N2f3		C2h3	N7f8
	N8f7	P7f1		R3f1	C2f2*a
	R9h8	R1h2		R3h7	N8f6
	R8f4	N8f7		R7f2	M7f5
	P3f1	P7f1		R7b3	N6f8
	R8h3	P3f1		N2f1	N8f6

	Red	Blue		Red	Blue
	K5f1	C2h6*[h]	**c.**	R7f2	C8f6
	K5h6	C8f6		C3h9	R7f9
	R1h2	R9f1		R7h2	N6f7
	R7h6	R2f8		S6f5	C2f5
	K6f1	N6f5		N7b8	R2f8
	C5b1	R2h4		C5h4	N7f6
	K6h5	R4b3		R2b6	N6b7
				C4b2	R2h5
a.	C3f7	S6f5		R2h5	R7h6
	R3h7	N8f6*[b,e]			
	C3b5	N6f4	**d.**	R7h5	R4b1
	C3h6	M3f5*[f]		R5h2	R4h3
	R7h2	N4f3		M3f5	N4f3
	C6b3	C2h3		K5h4	C2h6
	R2f2	C3f3			
	M7f9	R9h6	**e.**	R7f2	N6f8
	R1f1	R2f9		R7h2	N8f6
	R2h5	R2h4		N5f1	R9h7
	K5h6	R6f9		N2f1	C2h5
	C5b2	C3h4		C5f3	R2f8
	C6h5	R6h5		K5f1	N6f8
	K6f1	C4b6			
			f.	R7b1	R9h7
b.	C3b8	R9h7*[c]		N2f1	N4f3
	N2f1	N6f4		C6b3	C2f4
	R7f2	R7f8		R1f1	C8f5*[g]
	C5h6	R7h4		N7b9	R7f9
	S4f5	M3f5*[d]		R7f3	R2f7
	R7b3	C2h5		C5f4	R2h6
	R1h2	R4b1		S6f5	C2h4
	R2f7	R4h7		S5f4	C4h8
	K5h4	C5h6		K5h6	C8h1
	R7h6	R2f5		S4b5	C8f2
	R2f2	S5b6			
			g.	C5b1	R7f7
				C5f1	R7h5

Red	Blue		Red	Blue
M3f5	C8h3	**a.**	M3f1	C2f3
R7h4	C3f2		C3h2	R7f5
K5f1	C2h4		M1f3	P5f1*[b]
K5h6	C3h1		P5f1	P5f1
			C5f5	K5h6*[d]
h. C5f4	S6f5		S4f5	R2f3
R7h4	R2f8		R1h4	C8h6
K5f1	R9h6		C2f3	N8f6
C5b1	C8f2		R4h3	C6h7
C3f3	C8f3			
C3b3	N6f5	**b.**	C2h6	R2f3
C3f1	C6f5		C6b4	R2h7*[c]
R4f5	K5h6		M3b1	R7f3
N1b2	N5b6		R1h3	N8f6
C3b1	R2h4		N3b1	N6f5
R1f2	N6b5		M7f5	R7h5
R1h2	N5f3		M1f3	C2h5
			S4f5	R5h9
2. C8h5	N2f3		N1f3	R9h4
N8f7	P7f1		K5h4	R4h6
R9h8	R1h2		K4h5	C8f5
R8f4	N8f7			
P3f1	R7f1	**c.**	S4f5	R7f2
R8h3	P3f1		R1h4	N3f5
C2h3	N7f8		R4f5	N5b7
C3f7	S6f5		R4h5	N8f7
N2f3	M3f5		R5h6	N7f9
C3b3	R9h7*[a,e]		C5h1	R7f2
R1f1	C2f3		M7f5	R7h5
R1h8	P3f1		C1f4	R5b1
R3h7	R7f3			
R8f3	R2f5	**d.**	C2h6	C2f2
R7h8	R7f4		M3b5	R2f3
N7b5	R7h6		C6b3	R2h5
R8h3	N8f9		C6h4	R5b1

	Red	Blue
	N3f4	N8b6
	N4f3	K6h5
	R1h2	R5h7
	R2f4	N3f5
e.	P5f1	N8b6
	R3b1	N6f5
	R3h5	P7f3
	N3f4	R7f2
	R5f1	N3f4
	R5f2	N4f6*f
	R5f1	N6f4*i
	R5h2	C2h5
	S4f5	R7h6
	R2f2	R6b5
f.	C5f5	S5b6
	R5b2	C8f1*g,h
	C5b1	N6b7
	R5b2	C8h5
	R5f4	C2h5
	M3f5	R7b1
	N7f5	R7h5
g.	C5b2	R7b1
	R5h4	R7h5
	M3f5	C8h5
	S4f5	C5f4
	M7f5	R5f3
	R1h4	C2f7
	N7b8	R5f1
	S6f5	R2f9
h.	M3f5	R7b3
	R1h2	C8h5

	Red	Blue
	S4f5	N6f5
i.	R1f1	R7h6
	R1h6	K5h6
	S6f5	N4f5
3.	C8h5	N2f3
	N8f7	P7f1
	R9h8	R1h2
	R8f4	N8f7
	P3f1	P7f1
	R8h3	P3f1
	C2h3	N7f8
	C3f7	S6f5
	C3h6	K5h4
	N2f3	M3f5*a,b
	N3f4	K4h5
	N4f5	N3f5
	C5f4	R2h4*k
	R3f4	N8b7
	C5b2	R9h8
	R1f1	C8f6
	R1f1	C8h3
	R1h4	R4f8
	R4f4	K5h4
	S4f5	R8f9
	R4h3	C3b2
	M7f9	C3h9
	C5h4	R8b2
	N7b8	R4b3
	C4b2	C9f3
	C4b2	R8h5
	N8f7	C2f7
	M9b7	R4f3
	R3b5	R5f3

	Red	Blue		Red	Blue
a.	R3h6	K4h5		P5f1	C8f1
	N3f4	N8f6		R3b4	R4h7
	R6h4	C8f5			
	R4b2	C8b1	**d.**	C5f4	R4f3
	R4f1	R9h8		M3f5	C7f5
	R1f1	C8f3		R3b4	N8f6
	R1h3	R2h4			
	S6f5	R4f8	**e.**	R3f2	P3f1
				P7f1	C2h8
b.	R1f1	R9h6*c		R3h2	R4f4
	R1h6	K4h5*h		R8h7	R4h7
	R6f7	R2h4		M3f1	R7f3
	R6h7	R4f7*i,j		S5b4	R7h5
	N7b9	C2f6		M7f5	N6f7
	R3f4	R6f8		S6f5	S7b8
	C5f4	K5h4			
	S4f5	R4f1	**f.**	R3b4	N6f4
	C5f2	N3b5		C2h6	C8f5
	R3h5	R6h5		M3f5	R4h6
	S6f5	C2f1			
	S5b6	R4f1	**g.**	R8h7	R4h6
	K5f1	R4b1		R7h6	N6f8
	K5f1	N8f7		C2f3	R6f4
	K5h4	C8f5		R6b6	N8f7
	N3b2	R6h4		C2f4	R6h8
				R6h3	R8f8
c.	R3f2	C8h7		N7f6	K5h6
	R1h6	K4h5		S5f4	R6h4
	R6f7	R2h4		K5h4	R4f1
	R6h8	C2f2*d		K4f1	R4b1
	S4f5	C7f5		K4b1	N7b5
	R3b4	N8f6*e		N6b5	R8h5
	R3f6	P3f1			
	P7f1	C2h8	**h.**	R3f4	C8h7
	C5h2	R4f4*f,g		N3f2	R2h4

	Red	Blue			Red	Blue
	R6h8	C2f2			C5f2	N6f5
	R8f3	P3f1				
	R8h7	C2h7	**m.**		R4f1	K5h6
	R3h2	C7f7			R1f2	R4f3
	S4f5	C7h8			C5h1	N6f7
	C5h3	R6f8			C1f3	C2f3
	R2f1	C7b4			N7b8	R4h6
	R7f3	N8b9			S6f5	C8h7
	R2h1	N9b8			R1b2	N7f8
	R1b1	K5h6			R1h2	R6h7
	S5f4	R6b1			M3f5	C7h8
	N2f3	N8f7				
	C3f5	R4f8	**4.**		C8h5	N2f3
					N8f7	P7f1
i.	N7b8	C2f6			R9h8	R1h2
	R3f4	R4f1			R8f4	N8f7
	C5f4	K5h4			P3f1	P7f1
	S6f5	N8b6			R8h3	P3f1
	R3h2	N3f5			P7f1	C8b1*[a]
					C2h3	C8h7*[f]
j.	R3f4	R4h3			R3h4	N3f4
	C5f4	K5h4			R4h6	N7f6
	C5f2	N8b6			C3f7	R9h7
	R3h2	N3b5			R6f1	N6f7
					N2f1	N7f8*[i,j]
k.	R3f1	C2f2			S4f5	P3f1*[l]
	R3f3	N8b6*[l]			R6h7	C2h5
	R3h4	R9h6*[m]			R7b1	C7h6*[m,n,q]
	R4h1	P3f1			R1h2	R2f8
	R1b2	P3f1			R7h2	C5h3
					R2h7	C3h8
l.	R3b1	C8f2			R2h1	C6f8
	R1h2	C8h5			R1f1	R7f9
	M3f5	R9h6				
	P5f1	R4f3	**a.**		N2f1	C8h7

Red	Blue		Red	Blue
R3h6	P3f1		R3f2	R9f1
R6h7	N3f4		N1f3	R9h4
R7h6	C2h3*b			
R6f1	C3f7*e	**e.**	K5f1	R9h8
S6f5	C3h1		R1h2	R8f4
K5h6	M3f5		R6b1	R2f8
R6b1	R9h8		R6b3	R2h4
C2h4	R8f4		K5h6	C3h6
N7f8	N7f6		R2f1	R8h2
C5f4	C7h5		S6f5	R2f4
C4h8	R2h3		K6f1	C6b2
b.	M7f9	R2f4	**f.**	R3h6	N7f6
C2h4	M3f5		R6h3	N6b8
R1h2	C7h4		R3f2	C2f1
R6h3	C4h3		R3b3	C7f6
N7f6	R2f4		N2f3	P3f1
C5h7	N4f2*c		P5f1	N8b6
M3f5	C3f6*d		N7f5	P3h4
C4h7	N2f1		N5f3	M7f5
S4f5	R9f1		R3h7	R9h7
R3h4	N1f3		rNf5	P4h5*g
K5h4	C3b1		R7f4	P5f1*h
R2f7	C3h6		C5f4	S4f5
S5f4	R2f1		N3b5	R7f3
M5b7	R2b4		C5h9	C2h5
			M3f5	R7f3
c.	C7f6	C3f7		R7b4	N6f5
S6f5	C3h1			
M9f7	R9f1	**g.**	C5f2	N3f4
C7h2	N7f6		C5h6	C2f6
			M3f1	N4f6
d.	N6b7	N2f3		R7b1	rNf5
C4h7	R2b1		R7h4	R2f6
M9b7	R2h3		N5b6	N6f4

	Red	Blue			Red	Blue
	R4h3	N5f6			S4f5	C2b2
					M7f9	C7f6
h.	N3b5	R7f6			C5f4	C7h1
	N5f7	R7h3			C5b2	C1f2
	R7b1	C2f6			N7b8	C2h3
	N7f5	R3h5				
	N5b3	R5h4	**l.**		C5f4	C2h3
	S4f5	N6f7			C5b2	C3f5
	R1h2	C2h1			M3f5	R2f6
					R6h5	C7h5
i.	S6f5	C2f7			R5h8	C5f5
	N7b8	R2f9			R8b2	C3b1
	C5f4	R2h3				
	R6b5	R3b3	**m.**		R7h2	C5h3
	P5f1	C7h2			M7f9	C6f8
	P7f1	R7f5			R1f1	C6h4
	P5f1	R3b2			R1h2	C4h1
	P5h6	R7h5			S5b4	C3f4
	R1f1	N8b6			rRh3	R7f8
	R1h4	R3f3			N1b3	R2f9
	P6f1	C2h6			K5f1	R2b1
	C5h4	R3f1			K5b1	R2h7
					R2h8	R7f1
j.	R1f1	R7h8*k			C5f4	R7b2
	C5f4	C2f6				
	S4f5	P3f1	**n.**		R7h4	C5h3*o,p
	C5b2	P3f1			M7f9	C6h3
	M3f5	N8b6			C5f4	R2f7
	S5f4	R8f9			R4f3	R2h3
	M5b3	R8h7			M3f5	K5f1
	K5f1	C2h9			R1h2	R7h8
	R6h5	C7h5			R2h3	R8f7
	R5h8	M3f5				
			o.		N7f8	C6h3
k.	R6h7	C2f6			M7f9	R2f4

	Red	Blue			Red	Blue
	C5f4	R2h5	**5.**		C8h5	N2f3
	R4f2	R7f7			N8f7	P7f1
	M3f5	R7h5			R9h8	R1h2
	P5f1	fRh1			R8f4	N8f7
	C5h7	C3f2			P3f1	P7f1
	R4h7	N8b6			R8h3	P3f1
	K5h4	N6b5			N2f1	C8b1
	N8b9	R5h6			C2h4	C8h3
	S5f4	R6f3			R1h2	R9f1*[a,c,e,x]
	K4h5	R6h5			R3f2	R9h4
					C4h3	R4f7
p.	N7f6	C6h3			C3f5	P3f1*[z,a']
	M7f9	R2f8			P7f1	C3f4*[c',d']
	C5h7	C3f6			N7f8	C2h7
	N6b7	R7f7			R3f1	M3f5
					N8f7	R4b5
q.	C5f4	C6h5*[r]			N7f9	R2f9
	C5f2	N8b6			C5h3	R2h3
	K5h4	C5h6			S4f5	C3h2
	R7h4	S4f5			N9f7	R4b2
	S5f4	R7f5			R2f8	C2f4
	R4f1	R7h3			K5h4	N3f4
	M3f5	R3f2			R2h6	R3b8
	K4h5	R2f6			K4f1	R3h4
	P5f1	C6f5				
	R4b3	R2h4	**a.**		R2f6	C3h7
					R3h8	N3f4
r.	C5b2	R2f8			R8h6	C2f2
	M3f5	R2h4			P7f1	N7f6
	R7h6	C5f4			R2h5	M3f5
	R6b3	fCf2			R6h3	P3f1
	S5f4	fCh4			R3h7	R9h8
	R6h5	N8b6			R5h3	C2b2*[b]
	K5h4	C5h6			R3b2	C2h3
					M7f9	C7h3

Red	Blue		Red	Blue
R7h5	N4f3		R3h4	K5h6
R5f1	C3f5		R2f8	K6f1
C4h7	C3f6		R2b1	K6b1
R5h4	N3f5		R2h6	N5f3
			N5b6	C3f3
b. R7f1	N6b7		K5f1	R2f7
R3h6	C7f8		M3f5	C2b1
S4f5	N4f6			
		f.	P1f1	C3f5
c. P1f1	P9f1		M7f9	N7f6
P1f1	R9f3		R6b3	P3f1
R2f8	N3b5*d		M9f7	C2f7
R2b4	P3f1		S6f5	R2f6*g
P7f1	C2f3		N1f2	N6f7*h
N7f8	C3f8		C5f4	C2h1
S6f5	R2f5		R6h9	R2f3
P7f1	R2f4		S5b6	N4f5
R3h8	R2h1			
R2h6	R9h3	**g.**	R2f5	C2h1
			R6h9	N4f6
d. R2b2	P3f1		R2h4	N6f5
P7f1	C2f7			
C5f4	N7f5	**h.**	N2f3	N7f5
R2h5	C3f6		M7b5	C3h1*i
R3f5	R2f8		N7f9	C2h1
			R6f1	R2h1
e. R3h8	N3f4		R2f5	R1h3
R8h6	R9h4*f,j,r		R6h7	R4h2
R2f6	C3f2			
R2b5	C3f3	**i.**	R6h9	N4f5
M7f9	N7f6*t,v		N7h9	R2h3
R6h3	N4f5		N9b7	N5f3
R3f5	N6f4*w		R9h7	N3f5
N7f5	C2f7			
M9b7	N4f5	**j.**	C4h3	M7f5*k

Red	Blue
R6h3	C3f5
M7f9	N4f5
R3h8	N5f7
R2f3	P3f1
M7f9	N7b6

k.

Red	Blue
N1f3	C3f5*l
M7f9	C3h7
C3f5	C2h7*m
R6h3	M5f7
R3f1	C7h3*p
N7f6	N4f6
N6f5	N6f5
M3f5	R4f2

l.

Red	Blue
C3f5	C3f3
S6f5	C2h7
N3f4	P3f1
C5f4	S4f5
R6b2	C7h6
N4f2	C3h1
N2f4	K5h4
C5h2	N4f6
R2f9	R2f9
N7b6	R4f6
S5f6	C1h4
S4f5	C4h7
S5b6	N6f7
R2h4	K4f1
C5f1	R2h4

m.

Red	Blue
C5f4	S4f5
R6h3	R2f3*n,o
R3f3	R2h5
R3b4	N3f4

Red	Blue
M9b7	R4f6
N7b8	K5h4
S4f5	R4h2
N8f9	N3f2

n.

Red	Blue
R2f6	C7h1
R3f3	C1h2
C5h3	N4f6

o.

Red	Blue
C5b2	N4f3
R3f3	N3f1
R2f1	C7b3
R2h9	N1b3
R3h5	R4f6
R5h8	R2h5

p.

Red	Blue
C5f4	C3f5
R2f7	N4f5*q
M3f5	C3f2
M9b7	N5f3
S4f5	C7h5
K5h4	R4h6
K4h5	R2f3
C5b2	R2h6

q.

Red	Blue
S4f5	R2f3
C5b2	R4f4
R3h5	S4f5
C5f4	N5b7

r.

Red	Blue
C5h6	N7f6*s
R6h8	N4f5
C6h5	P3f1
P7f1	S4f5
N7f5	N6f5

Red	Blue		Red	Blue
C5f4	C2h5	**v.**	R6h8	N4f5
R8f5	N5f3		R2f4	P3f1
			R8h7	S4f5
s. R6b1	C2f4		R7b1	N5f3
P7f1	C2h5		R7b1	C2f7
C6f3	C5b2		S6f5	N6f4
C4f2	C3f4		R7h8	R2f7
R6f1	C3f4		C4h8	R4h3
K5f1	P3f1		S5f6	R3f8
			K5f1	R3b1
t. R6b3	P3f1*u		K5b1	N4f6
C5f4	N6f4			
R2f6	N4b3	**w.**	R3h4	K5h6
R2h5	S4f5		R2f8	K6f1
R5h7	N4b5		R2b1	K6b1
R6f7	C3b4		R2h6	N5f3
R6b2	C3f5		C4h7	C3h5
R6h5	C2f7			
M9b7	R2f8	**x.**	R3h6	N3f2*y
S4f5	C3h1		R6f2	C3f5
R5h7	R2h3		M7f9	C3h2
M3f5	C1f2		R2f4	R9h3
u. M9f7	C2f7	**y.**	R2f6	M3f5
N7b8	C3f3		R2h4	P3f1
S6f5	R2f9		R6h7	C2h3
M7b9	C3b1		R7h8	R9h4
R6b1	R4h2		R4b2	R4f7
R6h8	R2f8		P1f1	S4f5
S5b6	R2b1		N1f2	R2h4
R2f4	C3f1			
S6f5	C3h1	**z.**	C5f4	N3f5
R2h4	N4f3		R3h5	C2h5
S5f6	N3f4		S4f5	C3f5
			M7f9	R2f7

Red	Blue		Red	Blue
C3b6	R4b4		K5f1	N2f4
R2f2	R2h1			
R2h3	M7f9	e'.	R3h5	S4f5
P1f1	C3h2		R5h8	N2f3
R5h8	P3f1			
N1f2	P3f1	6.	C6h5	N2f3
R8b3	R4f5		N8f7	P7f1
			R9h8	R1h2
			R8f6	N8f7
a'. C3h8	P3f1*b'		R8h7	C2b1*a
C5f4	N3f5		R7h8	N7f6
R3h5	C3h5		P7f1	P7f1
C8h2	R2f3		N2f1	P7f1
R5b2	P3f1		C2h4	M7f5
S4f5	R2h6		R1h2	C8f1
N1f3	R6f3		R8f1	C2h8
N3f2	M3f5		R8f2	C8f8
R5h7	C5f5		R8b2	C8h9
M3f5	S4f5		R8h7	P7f1*h
			C5h3	R9h7
b'. C5h3	M3f5		C3b1	C8f4
C8h5	M7f5			
C3h2	P3f1	a.	N2f1	C2h3
C2f7	M5b7		R7h6	R2f8
R3f3	K5f1		P7f1	C3f4
N1f3	K5h4		N7f6	N3f2*b
S4f5	N3b5		R6h7	R2h3
			M7f9	N2f4
c'. M7f9	C2f7		R7b2	R3b3
N7b8	R2f9		M9f7	C8f4
S4f5	C3f3		P5f1	C8h1
C5f4	C3h5		M7b9	C1h5
C5b5	S4f5		S4f5	R9f1
			R1h2	R9h6
d'. N7b8	N3f2*e'		M9f7	C5h3*f
C5f4	R4f1			

	Red	Blue
	M7b9	R6f7
	M9b7	N4f2
	C5h8	C3h5
	M7f5	K5f1
	C2h4	N2f4
	C4h6	K5h6
b.	R6h8	C8f4*c,e
	N6f5	C8h5
	S6f5	M7f5
	N5f3	R2f1
c.	C5f4	C8h5
	C5b1	N2f4*d
	C2f4	N4f6
	C2h5	N6b5
	C5b3	C3h5
	C5h8	N5f3
d.	R8h5	S6f5
	R5h7	M7f5
	R7b2	R9h6
e.	P3f1	C8h1
	C5f4	N7f5
	R8h5	M3f5
	N6f4	N2f3
	M3f5	N3f5
	M7f5	C1f3
	M5b7	R2h3
f.	S5f6	C3f3
	S6f5	C3h1
	C2h3	R6h2*g
	K5h4	R2f8

	Red	Blue
	K4f1	R2b4
	R2f7	R2h3
	R2h3	N4f5
g.	K5h6	R2f8
	K6f1	N7f6
	R2f4	P7f1
	R2h3	N4f5
	M7b5	N6f5
h.	C5f4	S6f5
	C4f2	P7h6
	N1f3	R9h7
	N3f4	R7f9
	N4f2	R7b6
	S4f5	P6f1
7.	C8h5	N2f3
	N8f7	P7f1
	R9h8	R1h2
	R8f6	N8f7
	N2f1	M7f5
	R8h7	N7f6*a,b
	P7f1	C2f4
	C5f4	S6f5
	C5b1	C2h3
	R7h4	C3f3
	S6f5	C3h1
	R4b1	C8f2
	R4h3	C8h5
a.	R7b2	S6f5
	R7h4	R9h6
	C2h4	N3f4
	R4b1	N4f5

	Red	Blue
	N7f5	C8f4
	P3f1	C8h5
	S4f5	C2f7
	C4f3	C5h1
	P7f1	C1f3
	K5h4	R2f8
	K4f1	C2h4
	N1b2	C4h6
b.	R7h8	C8f4
	C2h4	N6f5*c
	N7f5	C8h5
	S4f5	N3f4
	R8h5	S6f5
	R5b1	R9h6
	K5h4	C2f7
	C5h6	R2f8
	K4f1	C5h9
	R1h2	N4f5
	C6h5	N5f3
c.	R1h2	N5b4
	R8h7	C8h3
	M7f9	S6f5
	R2f4	R9h6
	S4f5	C2f7
	N7b8	R2f9
	R2f6	C3h5
	R6f1	R6f7
	R6b2	C5f2
	K5f1	K5h6
	C5h7	M5f3
	R7b1	N3f2
	P1f1	M3f5
	R7b1	N2f1

	Red	Blue
	R6h9	R6f1
	K5b1	R6f1
	K5f1	R2h4
8.	C8h5	N2f3
	N8f7	P7f1
	P9h8	R1h2
	R8f6	N8f7
	N2f1	M7f5
	R1f1	P3f1*a
	R1h4	N3f4
	R8h6	N4f3
	R4f5	S6f5
	R6h8	N3b4
	R4h3	P3f1
	R8b1	N4f6
	R3f1	C2h7
	R8f4	P7f1
	P3f1	C7f7
	S4f5	R9h7
	C5h4	R7f5
	M7f5	N6f5
	C2h5	C7h9
	C4h2	R7f4
	S5b4	R7b2
	C2b2	R7h5
	S6f5	R5h9
	N7b8	C8h7
	C2h3	R9h7
	C3h2	R7h2
a.	R8h7	N7f6
	R1h4	C2f2
	R4f3	S6f5
	P1f1	R9h6

	Red	Blue			Red	Blue
	S4f5	R2f2			R9h6	N8f7
	R7h9	N3f4			K5f1	C2h5
	R4h8	N6f7*b,d			M7f5	R2f6
	C2h3	N7f9			R6b5	R2b5
	M3f1	P3f1			R2b3	P7f1
	R8h7	N4f6			N2b1	N7b9
	C3h2	C8f3			M3f1	R6h5
	R7f4	N6f8			K5h4	P7f6
	C5f4	C8f2			R6f4	R2f5
	R9h7	C8h5			N7b5	R2h4
	S5f4	C5b4			R6h7	K5h4
	R7h5	N8f6			R7h5	R5h7
	K5f1	C2h5			R2b5	P6f1
	R5b1	R2f6				
	K5f1	N6f8	**d.**	C5f4	P3f1
	S6f5	R6f7			R8h7	N4f6
					C5b2	C8h7*e,f
b.	C2h4	P3f1			M7f5	N7f8
	R8h7	N7f8			R7f5	C2h5
	R7h2	N8b6			R7b3	N6f5
	S5f4	R6f7			C5f3	S5f4
	R2f3	N4f6*c			M3f5	R6f9
	S6f5	R6f1			S5b4	N8b6
	N1f3	R6h7				
	N3f4	R7f1	**e.**	C2h4	N7f9
	S5b4	N6f7			M3f1	N6f8
	R2f2	S5b6			C4h2	C2h5
	C5f4	S4f5			R9h2	R6f6
	C5h4	C2f5			R2h3	R2f5
	M7f5	C2h1			R3f1	R2h3
	K5h6	N7f6			M7f5	C5f2
c.	N1f2	N6f8	**f.**	R9h2	N7b5
	R2f2	S5b6			P5f1	C7f7
	C5f4	S4f5				

Red	Blue		Red	Blue
C2h4	N6b8	**g.**	N7f5	C2h9
P5f1	C2f3*g		R2b1	C9f2
C4h8	R2f5		R2b5	C7h4
R2b1	R2h3		R2f3	C4b3
R2b5	C7h4		N5f4	C4h1
S5b6	R3h9		R2f3	C1f3
P5f1	R9b1		C5b6	R6h7
R7h5	P7f1		P5f1	R2f5

Central Cannon vs. Cross-Palace Cannon (5 games)

	Red	Blue		Red	Blue
1.	C2h6	C8h5		M3f5	P5f1*b
	N2f3	N8f7		R7h9	M3f1*c
	R1h2	R9f1		R9h8	P5h6
	R2f4	R9h4		C8f1	C5b4*d
	S6f5	N2f3		P7f1	N7f5
	R2h7	P5f1		N9f7	N5f4*e
	R7f2	R1f2		R8f2	C5h2
	C6h7	R4f7		R8h9	C2h3
	N8f9	C2f4		C8f6	S4f5
	R7f1	C2h5*a		N7f5	C3f5
	M3f5	C5h1*f			
	R9h8	C1h2	**b.**	R7b3	P5h4
	R8h9	R1h3		R7f5	R1h2
	C7f5	C5f5*g		R9h8	N7f5
	S5f4	C2h7			
	C8f1	C7b1	**c.**	P9f1	N7f5
	P7f1	C7h5		N9f8	N5f6
	C8h5	fCh7		P3f1	P7f1
	S4f5	R4b2		N8f7	P7f1
	C5b1	C7h5		N7f9	S4f5
	M7f5	R4h9		R9h8	P7f1
a.	N3f5	C5f4	**d.**	C8f6	S4f5

Red	Blue
R8f5	N7f5
P9f1	K5h4
N9f8	N5f3

e.

Red	Blue
C7h8	N4f3
M7f9	C5h8
S5b6	R4h7
R8h7	C8f7
S4f5	R7f1
S5b4	R7b3
S4f5	R7h3
C8f6	M1b3
R7f1	C8b5
S5b4	R3h2
R7f1	C8f3
R7b1	R2f1
C8h9	C2h5
S4f5	R5h7
K5h4	C8b3

f.

Red	Blue
N9b8	R1h3
C7f5	C5f5
S5f6	C5h2
R9f3	C2h7
N8f7	N7f5
C7b3	N5f7
P3f1	N7f5
S4f5	C7h5
K5h4	N5f7
P3f1	P5f1

g.

Red	Blue
S5b6	N7f5
C7b3	C2h7
C8f2	N5f7
C7h3	N7f5

Red	Blue
C3f5	S6f5
N3f5	C7h8

2.

Red	Blue
C2h6	C8h5
N2f3	N8f7
R1h2	R9f1
R2f4	R9h4
S6f5	N2f3
R2h7	P5f1
R7f2	R1f2
C8h7	N3f5
R7h8	P5f1*a
C7f7	S4f5*b
P5f1	C5f3*i
C6h5	N5f6
N3f5	C5f2
M7f5	N6f8*k
R8h4	C2f6
M5f7	N8f7
N5b4	R1h5*n
R9f2	R5h2
R9h6	C2h6
R4b5	R4f6

a.

Red	Blue
C6h5	N5f6
C5f2	S4f5
M7f5	N6f8
C7b1	C2f7
R8f3	R1h3

b.

Red	Blue
C6h5	N5f6*c,f
C5f2	N6f8*h
C5h4	N7f5
R8h5	N8f7
C4b3	C2f6

	Red	Blue			Red	Blue
	R9f1	R1h3			R8f3	N7f5
	R9h8	R3f4			N5f6	N5f4
					N6f5	R1h5
c.	P3f1	N6f7				
	C5f2	R4f7	g.	R9f1	R4h1
	N8f7	K5h4*d,e			N7b9	N7f5
	C5h9	N7b5			R8h5	C2f7
	C9f3	C5f3			M7f9	P5f1
	R8b2	N5b3			R5b4	R1h4
	M3f5	C2h5				
	C9f2	K4f1	h.	R8h4	C2f6
	R8f4	K4f1			C5h4	N8f7
	R8b1	C5h2			C4b3	R1h3
	P7f1	K4b1			C7h9	R4f7
	C7b2	N7f5				
	R9h8	C2f6	i.	K5h6	C2h4*j
	C7h2	N5f6			C6f6	N5f4
	C2b6	R4f1			S5f6	N4f3
	N7b6	C2h8			K6h5	C4h5
					R8h5	N7f5
d.	R9f1	R4b6			N8f7	R1h4
	M7f5	N7b5			K5f1	R4f5
	N7f5	C5f4			C6h9	N5f6
	R9b1	P1f1			K5h4	R4h6
	R8b2	N7f5				
				j.	R8h6	C4f5
e.	C7b2	R1b1			R6b4	R4f6
	R9f1	R1h4			S5f6	N5f6
	C7h3	C5f4			N3f5	C5h4
					S6b5	N6f4
f.	N3b1	R4f7			K6h5	R1h5
	N8f7	N6f5			N5f4	R5f2
	M3f5	P5f1*g			N4f3	C4h1
	N7f5	C5f5				
	S5f6	C2h5	k.	M5f7	R4f5*l

Red	Blue		Red	Blue
N8f7	N8f7		C5f2	C2f5*e
N5b4	C2h5		R7h8	C2h7
S5f6	N7f5		C7f7	S4f5
K5h6	N7b6		R8f3	C5f3
			P5f1	N5f7*g
l. N8f6	C2h5		R8b7	fNf5
R9f1	R1h4		R8h3	R1h5*h
C7h9	R4h5		R3h5	K5h4*i
R8f3	R4b2*m		R9h8	N5f6
C9h6	R5h3		S5f4	R4f1
S5f4	N7f5		K5f1	N7f5
M7b5	N5f4		R8f2	R5h4
M5f7	N8f7		K5h4	N5f6
K5f1	R3h5		R5f2	R4b3
			S4f5	R4h8
m. M7b5	R5h3		R8h6	N6f7
R8b9	R4f8			
R9h6	N8f7	**a.**	P5f1	C5f3
K5h6	C5h4		N3f5	C5f2
R6f6	S5f4		M3f5	C2h5
S5f6	N7f5		N5f4	C5f5
			S5f4	N5f4
n. C7b3	P7f1		N4b6	C5b6
C7h6	N7f6			
		b.	P3f1	C2f5
3. C2h6	C8h5		C5h8	P5f1
N2f3	N8f7		C8f7	R1h4
R1h2	R9f1		R7f3	N5f4
R2f4	R9h4		R7b2	S4f5
S6f5	N2f3		R7h6	S5f4
R2h7	P5f1		C8b2	C5f3
R7f2	R1f2		C8h7	P5f1
C8h7	N3f5			
C6h5	R4f7	**c.**	R7h8	C2h3
N8f9	P5f1*a,b,c		C7f5	R1h3*d

Red	Blue		Red	Blue
C5h7	P5f1		N3f4	S4f5
C7f5	P5h6			
C7h3	N5f4	**f.**	C5f3	M3f5
N3f5	P6h5		C7h5	N5f6
R8f1	C5f2		P5f1	C2h7
R8b5	P5h6		C5f1	R4b2
M3f5	P6f1		R7h4	N6f7
R9f1	R4h1		C5h4	N7f9
R8h6	N4f6		M7f5	P7f1
R6f1	P6h5		P5f1	R1h4
K5h6	N6f5		R9h8	P7f1
			R8f4	N7f8
d.	P5f1	N5f6	R4f2	C7f1
	C5f5	R3h5	N9b7	N9b8
	N3f5	R4b2		
	N5b4	R5f3	**g.**	C7h4	S5b4
	R9h8	R4h6		C4b8	N7f8
	N4f2	R6f3		
	K5h4	N6f7	**h.**	M3f5	N7f5
	K4f1	R5f3		C7b5	K5h4
	K4f1	N7b5		R9h8	fNb7
	rRf1	R5b2		R3h4	N5f4
	rRf3	R5f3		R8f2	N7f6
e.	N3b1	C2b1*f	**i.**	P5f1	N5b7
	N1f3	C5f3		P5h4	N7f8
	P5f1	N5f6		
	N3b1	C2h7	**4.**	C2h6	C8h5
	C7h5	C7h5		N2f3	N8f7
	N9b8	R1h4		R1h2	R9f1
	N8f7	R4h5		R2f4	R9h4
	R7h4	N7f5		S6f5	N2f3
	P5f1	N6f5		R2h7	P5f1
	M3f5	rRh3		R7f2	R1f2
	N1f3	C5b1		C8f4	C2b1

	Red	Blue		Red	Blue
	C6h5	C2h3*a		N3f4	C5f3*d
	C5f3	N7f5*j		P5f1	N5f4
	C8h5	C5f2		N7f5	R4b2
	R7h8	N3f4*l		N5b3	C3f1
	R8h7	R1h2*r		M1b3	fRh2
	P5f1	N4f2		R8h9	C3b2
	R7b2	C5h3		R4h3	C3h5
	R7f1	N2f4		M7f5	R2h3
	N8f9	R2f5		R9h6	N4f2
	R9f1	N4b3		C7h6	N2f3
				C6b5	R3h1
a.	R7h3	N3f5		R3h7	R4f6
	C8h7	R4f7			
	N8f7	C3h7	**d.**	N4f5	N7f8*e
	R3h4	R1h4		R4h3	C5b1*f
	R9h8	P5f1*b		R3b1	N8f7
	P5f1	N7f8*h		R3h5	N7f5
	R4h5	N8f6			
	R5b1	N6f8	**e.**	R4h2	N8f7
	C5h4	C7f6		P1f5	N7f5
b.	C5f2	C7f5*c	**f.**	R8f5	N8f6
	M3f5	C5f3		R3h4	N6f4
	P5f1	N5f4			
	M5f3	N7f8*g	**g.**	R4b1	N8f9
	R4h2	N4f3		R4b2	N9f8
	C7b4	N8f6		N7f5	R4b2
	C7f7	S4f5		C7b2	fRh3
	C7h9	K5h4		P9f1	P9f1
	R2b4	N6f7		R4b2	N8b9
	R2h3	C7h5		R4f2	N9f7
	S5f6	rRh8		R4h3	N7b5
	R3f1	R4b1		M3b5	R3h1
c.	M3f1	C7h3	**h.**	R4h3	N8f6*i

Red	Blue		Red	Blue
R3f2	N6f8		N3b2	N4f6
R3h4	C5h6		C5b2	R4f4*n
C5h4	N5b6		N8f9	fRh5*o
C4b1	R4b5		C5h7	N6f4*q
R8f5	R4h6		C7f5	K5f1
			R9h6	R5h7
i. C5f4	C5f3		M3f1	C7h5
M3f5	R4h6		N2f4	R7h6
R3h4	C7f6		N4f2	K5h6
N7f5	N6f5			
S5f4	R6h8	**m.**	N3b1	N4f6
R4h2	R8h4		C5b2	C7h9
C5h6	rRf1		R8b3	R4f2
			R8f1	rRf2
j. C5f2	C3f2		R8f1	C9f4
C5h9	N5f6*k			
R9f2	N6f8	**n.**	R8b3	R4h5
R9h4	R4h2		R8h5	R4h5
C8b4	N8f7		R5h3	R5f4
K5h6	C3h4		R3h7	C3h8
C8h5	M7f5		N2f1	N6f5
R4b1	R2f8		M3f5	R5f1
			N1b2	fRh8
k. N3b1	R4h2		N2f4	R8f1
N8f9	R2f2			
C9f2	R2b3	**o.**	R8b4	N6f8
R9h8	R2h1		N2f1	R5h7*p
R8f4	N6b4		R9h6	R4f8
R8h7	C3h2		K5h6	R7h4
P5f1	C2f5		K6h5	C7h9
N1f3	R1h2		C5h1	C3h5
P5f1	N4f2		R8h5	M3f5
			R5h8	C9h5
l. R8f2	R1h4		C1h5	rCh7
M7f5	C5h7*m			

	Red	Blue		Red	Blue
p.	R8f1	C7f5		R3h1	C2f5*b
	M5b3	R7h5		C6b2	R1h2
	R8h5	R4h5		R1h7	R4f7
				R7f1	P5f1
q.	R9h6	C3f5		P5f1	C2h5
	R8h6	C7f5		M3f5	C5f5
	M5b3	R5f2		S5f6	R2f8
	S4f5	N4f6			
	K5h4	C3h6	**b.**	M7f5	P5f1*c
				P5f1	N3f2
r.	N8f9	N4b3		N8f6	C2h5
	R7h9	R2f2		M3f5	C5f5
	R9b2	R4f7		K5h6	R1h2
	P5f1	N3f5		P5f1	N2f3
	P5f1	R2h5		R9h7	P3f1
	rRh8	N5f3			
			c.	R1h7	P5f1
5.	C2h6	C8h5		N3f5	C2h5
	N2f3	N8f7		M3f5	C5f5
	R1h2	R9f1		K5h6	C5h9
	R2f6	R9h4		R7h2	R4f5
	S6f5	N2f3		N5f4	C9h7
	R2h3	P5f1*a		R2b6	N3f5
	P3f1	N3f5*f		N8f6	R1f1
	N3f4	C2f1		R9h8	R1h6*d
	N4f5	N7f5*i		N4f2	R4h7
	C6h2	P5f1*l		R2h3	N5f4*e
	P5f1	N5f4		R8h7	N4f5
	R3f3	C2f6*s		C6h3	R7f1
	R9h8	N4f3		R3h1	R7h6
	M7f5	N3f2		K6h5	fRh8
	C2f7	R1f2		N2b3	N5b7
				K5h6	R8b2
a.	C8f4	P3f1			
	C8h1	N7f9	**d.**	R8f6	N5f6

Red	Blue			Red	Blue
N4f2	R4h3			K6f1	R1h4
N6f8	C7h2			S5f6	R4f3
R8b4	N6f7				
R2h3	R3f3	**h.**		C8h4	N6f8
K6f1	N7b5			C6h2	R1f3
C6h5	N5f3			R9f2	R1h2
				N8f7	C2b1
e.	R8f2	C7h2		C4f2	C2h5
	R3f3	R6f8		P5f1	R2h4
	S5b4	N4f3		R9h8	R4f5
				R8f3	C5h6
f.	C8f4	P3f1		P4h3	C6f3
	N3f4	P1f1			
	N4f5	R4f2	**i.**	C6h5	R4f7
	P3f1	R4h5		N8f9	R1f2*j,k
	R3h5	N7f5		C8h6	N5f3
	P3h4	P5f1*g		R3h7	C5f4
	P4f1	N5f6		R7b1	R1h5
	C8h5	S4f5		R9h8	C2h7
	P5f1	N6f8		M3f1	C7h8
	C6h2	K5h4			
	M7f5	C5f3	**j.**	P7f1	P5f1
	N8f6	R1f3		C5f2	C5f3
	N6f5	R1h4		P5f1	N5f6
	R9h8	C2h1		R3h7	C2f3
	R8f4	C1f4		C8h5	C2h5
	R8h5	C1f3		N9f7	R4b2
	S5f6	N8f6		N7f9	R1h6
g.	P5f1	N5f6*h	**k.**	P5f1	N5f3
	C8b3	C2h4		R3h7	N3f4
	N8f7	P3f1		R7h8	C5f3
	P7f1	N6f8		R8b2	N4f3
	C6h5	N8f7		C8h6	R4h5
	K5h6	R1f3		K5h6	R5f1

	Red	Blue			Red	Blue
	K6f1	R1h4		**o.**	P7f1	R1h6
					N7f5	P5f1*p
l.	C2f7	N5f4			M5b7	P5f1
	R3f3	C5f4*m			P7f5	C2h7
	C8h5	N4f2			R3h2	N4f5
	N8f9	R1f2			M3f5	C7f3
	C2h4	R1h4			M5b3	R6f7
m.	M7f5	R1f2*n		**p.**	R3b4	N4f6
	N8f6	N4f5*q			R3h6	N6f7
	N6f5	N5f3			K5h6	R6f7
	N5b6	R4f7				
	C2b8	N3f1		**q.**	M3f5	R4f7*r
	C8h5	M3f5			R9h6	R4h2
	C2h6	P5f1			C2h4	R1h6
					C4b1	K5f1
n.	C2h4	R4h6			R3h6	P5h4
	C4h6	K5b1			C4f1	C5h8
	N8f6	C2f3*o				
	N6f5	C2h5		**r.**	C2h4	R1h6
	C8f6	R6f7			C4h6	K5f1
	R3b1	K5b1			R9h6	K5h6
	C6b1	R1h2			C6h4	R6f7
	C8h9	M3f1			C4b9	R4h5
	R9h7	R2f6				
	R3f1	R6b8		**s.**	M7f5	C5f5
	R3h4	K5h6			M3f5	N4f5
	K5h6	C5f2			C8h6	N5f7
	S4f5	P5f1			K5h6	C2h6
	M5f7	R2h5			R9f2	R1h2

Central Cannon vs. Cross-Palace Knight (3 games)

	Red	Blue		Red	Blue
1.	M3f5	C8h5		N2f4	N8f7

Red	Blue		Red	Blue
N4f6	R9h8		C5h6	P7f1
C2h3	C5f4		N8f7	N7f8
S4f5	C5h4		R9h8	N8f7
R1h4	C2f2*a,b		R4b5	R8f9
R4f3	C2h1		S5b4	N7f9
C8h9	C1h5		R8f1	R8b1
N8f7	R8f9		S4f5	R8h7
R4b3	R8h6			
K5h4	R1f1	**c.**	C3h2	C8h1
R9h8	R1h6		N8f9	C4h2
C3h4	R6h8		C2h3	C2b4
K4h5	R8f8		R9h8	C2h5
C4b2	S6f5		R4f7	R1f2
R8f4	C4h9		S5b4	C5f5
N6f7	R8b4		R4h9	C1h5
rNf5	P3f1		N6f5	N2f1
			M7f5	R8f7
a. C8f2	C2h5		C3f4	R8h5
C8h5	R1f1		S4f5	R5b2
N8f7	R8f7			
C3f4	R1h8	**d.**	R4h2	R8f9
C3f3	S6f5		S5b4	R1f2
R9h8	M3f5		N8f7	R1h4
C5b1	R8f2		C6h5	M3f5
R8f9	N7f6		R9h8	N2f4
C5f1	N6f7		S6f5	R4f4
R8b5	N7f5		C5f1	P7f1
M7f5	C5f3		R8f5	N7f8
			R8f3	N4f6
b. C8f1	C2h8*c		R8b3	N8f9
C8h6	C8f5*d		C3b2	P5f1
R4f7	C8h9			
C6h5	M7f5	**2.**	M3f5	C8h5
N6f5	N2f3		N2f4	N8f7
N5f6	R1f1		N4f6	R9h8

	Red	Blue			Red	Blue
	C2h3	C5f4			N7b6	P5h4
	S6f5	C5h4			N6f8	R1h2
	C8f1	C4h2			P8h9	R2f6
	N6f8	P5f1*a			R1h2	N5f6
	P7f1	P5f1*b			C3h4	P4f1
	P7f1	R8f4				
	N8b6	P5h4	c.	N8b6	N7f5
	P7f1	P4f1			R9h8	N2f3
	N6f8	R8h2			R8f6	R1h2
	N8f6	C2f7*f			R8h7	P5f1
	M7f9	R2f4*h			N7b6	R8f7
	C3b1	R2h5			C3f4	P5f1
	S4f5	C2h9			M7f5	R8h5
	M9b7	R1f1			N6f5	N5f4
	R9h8	R1h8				
	R8f9	R8f8	d.	N8b6	N1f3
	S5b4	R8b1			N6f5	N7f5
	C3b1	P4f1				
				e.	N7f8	R4b3
a.	N8f9	C2h5			P7h8	P5f1
	P7f1	P5f1				
	P7f1	N2f3	f.	S5b6	C2h4*g
	P7f1	N3f5			N6f8	C4h1
	P7h6	N5f6			M7f9	R1f1
	N8f7	S6f5			N8f6	N2f1
	C3h4	P5f1			P7f1	R1h4
	R9h8	M3f1			N6f4	R4h6
	R8f6	R1h3			N4b5	R6f6
b.	rNf7	C2h5*c	g.	K5h6	R2h4
	P7f1	R8f4			R9h8	R4f1
	P7f1	N2f1*d			R8f8	P4f1
	P7f1	R8h4			R1f1	R1f2
	N8b6	N7f5*e			R1h4	P4h5
	P7h8	P5f1			K6h5	R1h4

Red	Blue		Red	Blue
S4f5	P5h6		M3f5	C8f3

	Red	Blue		Red	Blue
h.	R1h2	R1f1	b.	C3h7	P5h4
	R2f7	C2h6		P9f1	C4h5
	S5b4	R1h5		C7h6	P4f1
				C7f5	P4f1
3.	M3f5	C8h5		C7b1	N5f7*c,d
	N2f4	N8f7		P3f1	P4f1
	N4f6	R9h8		R8b2	R8f1
	C2h3	C5f4			
	S6f5	C5h4	c.	R8h4	P4h5
	C8h7	C2h5		M7f5	R8f1
	N8f9	N2f3		N9b7	R1h2
	R9h8	P5f1		P3f1	R8h5
	R8f4	R8f6			
	R1h3	N7f5*a	d.	K5h6	fCh4
	R8h6	R8h7		K6h5	P4h5
	C3f4	R7f3		M7f5	R1f2
	M5b3	C4h5		P3f1	R1h4
	M3f5	P5f1*e,g		P3f1	R4f1
	R6f4	P5h4		C7b1	R8h5
	R6h3	fCh7		N9b7	C4h9
	C3h7	C5h7		P3h4	R4f5
	R3h2	P4f1		C7h5	R5b2
a.	C3f4	P5f1*b	e.	R6h8	P5h4*f
	P3f1	M7f9		C3h7	P4f1
	R3f3	P5f1		C7h6	P4f1
	R3h2	C4h8		C7f5	P4f1
	M5b3	P3f1		C7h6	R1h2
	P9f1	R1f1		R8h3	R2f8
	R8f2	R1h7			
	C3h2	R7f4	f.	C7f4	M3f1
	M7f5	P5f1		P9f1	S4f5
	C7h5	C5f5		R8f2	R1h4

Red	Blue		Red	Blue
C7h6	P4f1		C7f4	fCh4
N6b8	N5f6		C7h5	C5f5
C3h2	C5f1		M7f5	C4b3
R8b2	N6f5		C5b1	K5f1
			M5b7	C4f4

g. R6f2   P5h4